The Old Past Master

by Carl H. Claudy

Carl E. Weaver, Editor

Edited by Carl E. Weaver

Originally published in 1924 ByThe Masonic Service Association
Of the United States of America

ISBN: 978-0-9966341-2-0
Library of Congress Control Number: 2015948887

Foreword

Carl H. Claudy was a great thinker and storyteller in Masonry and is no doubt responsible for inculcating the tenets of Masonry to several generations of brothers. His style combines a sort of allegorical form with what is often discussion between a young Mason and an older, more seasoned and wise mentor, in this case, the Old Past Master. He is a wise man, and kind, and always unfailing when trying to communicate a lesson or general truth to his younger brother. The Old Past Master reminds me of other wise heroes of my time in popular culture. He is like Yoda, Obi-Wan Kenobi, Master Po, and Sam the Lion all rolled into one.

Claudy was a writer and editor by trade and excelled as a journalist for the New York Herald. He wrote books about aviation and photography but we in the Craft know him best for his many books and articles on Freemasonry. He wrote as many as 350 Short Talks for the Masonic Service Association over the years and was heralded as an expert on Masonry. He became a Master Mason in Harmony Lodge No. 17 in the District of Columbia in 1908, served as its master, and became Grand Master of Masons in 1943. He was also a 33° Scottish Rite Mason and an honorary grand master of North Dakota, as well as being an honorary member of many subordinate lodges.

The reason I chose to republish this book is because it communicates truths and wisdom in simple, obvious ways we can all understand. Claudy's young Masons present problems, sometimes a sort of straw man, and his Old Past Master proceeds to explain how to think about these issues while keeping the Masonic principles of faith, hope and charity in the forefront of the conversation. Especially important is that the lessons are never communicated in a harsh or pedantic style, but one full of warmth and brotherly love, communicated in a conversational tone.

Claudy's story "When Twice Two is Five" is the only problematic one I have encountered. In it he mentions that his grand lodge does not recognize "negro" Masons. This is largely a relic of a bygone age, thank goodness. In truth, there are still divisions between the traditionally all-white grand lodges and the Prince Hall grand lodges, which are primarily African-American. However, in most of America, these two systems have found amity and since have figured out how to live together in the Masonic bonds of friendship ad brotherly love. Many grand lodges have a number of subordinate lodges that are pretty well integrated. There are still a few holdouts, but this issue will, no doubt, be solved as more Masonic funerals happen. It is an issue of a fading generation, just as my own generation likely has issues that will die out with us. In addition, in this same story, Claudy describes lodges that do not admit Jews, Catholics, or foreigners. In my experience, I have yet to encounter any such lodges. These traditions must surely have died out over the years.

I hope you will enjoy these stories as much as I have.

Carl E. Weaver
Editor
8 August 2015

Preface

Masonry teaches the young and untried brother to apply to his elder brethren for instruction in the art and assures him that they will always be as ready to teach as his is ready to learn.

The author took this comforting assurance literally and seriously. To many "Old Past Masters" (and not all of them have been through the chairs!) ... he owes anything of Masonic wisdom which may have filtered through his pen to these pages. It is given to few to originate in this world; if to him has come opportunity to report to the many what would otherwise perhaps have been but the learning of the few, he is more than content, even if there be nothing within these pages which he can claim as his own.

A guidepost never gets anywhere, but it points the way!

Carl H. Claudy

CONTENTS

Brotherly Love

"Brotherly love?" commented the Old Past Master. "Oh, yes, the lodge is full of it. It is curious the way it manifests itself, sometimes, but when you dig down deep enough into men's hearts, you find a lot of it."

"A lot of them never show it, then," said the Very New Mason.

"Oh, no, certainly not! Men don't go around demonstrating their affection like a lot of girls, you know," answered the Old Past Master. "But you don't have to see a demonstration to know the feeling is there. The trouble with so many young Masons is their misunderstanding of the term 'brotherly love,' though high heaven knows the words are sufficiently easy to understand.

"'Brotherly,' now, means 'like a brother.' I know a lot of brothers hate each other, but they don't act like brothers. There have been cowardly soldiers, and forsworn ministers, and corrupt judges, but when you say a man is 'like a soldier,' you mean 'brave and true'; when you say he is 'good as a minister' you mean one who 'truly does his honest best.' When you say 'upright as a judge' you mean 'as straight as the best of judges.' And when I say 'brotherly' means 'like a brother,' I mean like a brother who is acting, as a good brother likes to act.

"As for 'love' there are more definitions than there are words in my mouth (which are several). But in connection with the 'brotherly' the word means that true affection which first considers the good of the person loved.

"Masonry teaches brotherly love. Many of its scholars are a long way from 100 per cent perfect in their lessons. But a lot could get an 'E' on their report card if the Lodge gave out evidence of scholastic standing!

"For instance, there was B'Jones. That is not his name, but it will serve. B'Jones undertook to do a piece of work for a hospital. It took him a year. At the end of the year his business was in shreds and tatters. He had one of those businesses that needs a man's personal attention.

"His attention had gone to his hospital, which, by the way, was built and flourishes, to the everlasting credit of his city. It ought to be called the B'Jones hospital, but it isn't.

"A lot of his brethren in his lodge got to know about B'Jones. They called a meeting, called it the B'Jones meeting, issued stock in the B'Jones association, bought the stock, started B'Jones off all over again, and let him pay them back as he could. All this, without B'Jones ever asking for help. Brotherly love, my son, in the best meaning of the word.

"There was poor old Smith. Smith, during his lifetime, came to the lodge every night. He wasn't very bright, was Smith. He couldn't learn the work and had no presence. Couldn't make a speech to save his life, so he never was called on at banquets. He never did anything audible, but he was always on committees and he always passed around refreshments and he attended every funeral, and he was always down ahead of the meeting to see if the room was clean, and if it wasn't, he'd sweep it out.

"He gave the best he had in service. Well, Smith died. Men do, you know; and awful lot have, already. At the funeral, we found out Smith left an invalid wife and two half grown children and no assets. It's the lodge's business to take care of such, and we did it. But three men in the lodge with more money than ability to keep it to themselves, subscribed enough cash to put the boy through a good business school and the girl through a normal school, so they could earn their own living. Charity? Nonsense! The lodge attended to the 'relief.' The three attended to brotherly love. They just remembered what old Smith was and how he gave, and so they turned to and gave. Actually, Smith did most of the loving. The three just acted in reflex to Smith's loving heart that so cared for his brethren and his Lodge he was always engaged in brotherly work.

"Do you know Brown? Brown runs a garage. Also, Brown ran a temperature until the doctors took him off to the hospital to cut out his something-or-other. Well, the garage was about to cash in. Garages don't run themselves, and there wasn't any one we could hire to run it. So six brothers of this lodge spent two hours a day each at the place, looking after it. We didn't do a very good job, I'm afraid: Brown says we are the worst garage keepers in the world, but we saved the shop from being wrecked and looted, and Brown thinks Masonry means something. One reason we did it was because of brotherly love in spirit of the fact that sitting around a cold garage selling gasoline is about the uneasiest apology for loafing I know!

"I could talk all night about it. But what's the use? Those to whom 'brotherly love' is just words won't listen to what I say and those who know what they really mean don't need to hear it."

"Well, I am glad I heard it!" answered the Very New Mason.

"Then," went the Old Past Master, "get it firmly fixed in your mind, young man, more than one man has gone into a lodge and curled his lip when he learned that he was supposed to be a brotherly lover, and turned around and wept when he found that he was being loved like a brother by men he didn't know cared what became of him.

"Masonry works miracles all the time, and the commonest of them and the one she works oftenest is teaching hard-hearted citizens to be soft-hearted Masons; teaching men the real meaning of the words 'brotherly' and 'love' until they, too, become teachers."

Attendance

"There are a lot of Masons in this old lodge tonight" began the Old Past Master. "See the new faces? Must be most two hundred. Pretty good attendance, what?"

"But is it a good attendance?" asked the Very New Mason. "Why, there must be six hundred members on the rolls. Seems a pity they can't all get out to enjoy this kind of an evening, doesn't it? Seems to me Masonry fails when she has so many on the rolls who don't come regularly to lodge."

"I don't agree with you!" answered the Old Past Master. "Masonry succeeds because she gets so many of her members to take an interest! True, she might... if she were a wizard... so interest every one of her devotees that all would crowd the lodge room every meeting night. Then, I think, there would be no use for Masonry, because the millennium would have come. But in place of being discouraged because only a third or a fourth of our members attend, I am always highly encouraged because so many do attend.

"You see, my brother, Masons are picked from the general body of men by two processes, and neither one of them works out for the very best interests of the Order. The first process is a man's making up his mind he wants to be a Mason. If we could go to the best men and ask them, we would get a lot better men than we do, of course. Equally, of course, we would vastly injure the Order by making it seek the man instead of the man seek its gentle philosophy. I wouldn't change that unwritten law for anything, but the fact remains that as the first selection of Masons is made by the profane, it isn't always for the best interests of the Order.

"The second selective work is done by committee. Now in theory every one appointed on a committee to examine a member is a sort of cross between a criminal lawyer, an experienced detective, a minister of the gospel, a super-perfect man, a well-read Mason and an Abraham Lincoln for judgment!

"But as a matter of fact most committeemen are just average men like you and me, and we do our work on committees in just an average sort of way, with the result that many a self-selected candidate slips into our ranks who has no real reason for being there. The theory is that all men become Masons because of a veneration of our principles. The fact is that a lot become Masons because their brother is one, or their boss is one, or they want to wear a pin and be a secret society member, or they hope it will help them in business.

"They get into the lodge and find it quite different from what they expect. They learn that they can't pass out business cards, that it doesn't help them because the boss belongs, and that they don't have to come to lodge to wear a pin. If they are the kind of men to whom Masonry doesn't appeal because of her truth, her philosophy, her Light, her aid in living, they wander away. They become mere dues-payers, and often, stomach Masons, who come around for the feed or entertainment.

"Don't let it distress you. It takes all sorts of people to make a world and it would be a very stupid place indeed if we were all alike. There is room in the world for the man who doesn't care for Masonry. He has his part to play in the world, as well as the man to whom Masonry makes great appeal. Do not condemn him because he has become a member of the fraternity and found it not to his liking. At least there is something in his heart which was not there before.

"And let me tell you something, my brother. There are many, many men who become Masons, in the sense that they join a lodge and pay dues, although they never attend, who do good Masonic work. There is Filby, for instance. Filby has been a member of this lodge twenty years and has never been in it, to my knowledge, since the day he was raised. I don't know why. I rather think he was frightened, and showed it, and has been afraid of being laughed at, now that he knows there was nothing to be frightened about. But there was never need for money that Filby didn't contribute; there was never a committee appointed to work on the Masonic Home that Filby didn't head. There was never any work to be done outside the lodge that Filby didn't try to help do it. He is a good Mason, even if he doesn't attend lodge.

"And there are lots of young men who join the fraternity and neglect their lodge in early years, who turn their hearts towards it in later years; boys who are too fond of girls and dances and good times to spend a moment in serious thought while they are just in the puppy age, who grow up finally to become thoughtful men, turning their hearts toward the noble teachings of this fraternity and becoming most ardent lodge members and attenders.

"Oh, no, my brother, never weep because we have but a portion of our membership at a meeting. Be glad we have so many; be happy that those who come, come so regularly and enthusiastically, be proud that there is such a large number of men content to sit through the same degrees year after year to learn what they can, let sink deeper the hidden beauties of the story, absorb a little more of that secret doctrine which lies behind the words of the ritual.

"Masonry is not for yesterday, for today, for tomorrow alone. She is for all the ages to come. The Temple Not Build With Hands cannot be built alone by you and me, nor in a day, nor yet a century. And remember that the stone rejected by the builder was finally found the most necessary of them all. Perhaps the man who doesn't come now to lodge may be the most earnest and powerful Mason of tomorrow. Only the Great Architect knows. Masonry is His work. Be content to let it be done His way."

"In My Heart"

"Why really does a man become a Mason?" asked the Very New Brother of the Old Past Master. "I know the prescribed answer to the question, of course. And doubtless every man who makes it thinks he tells the truth. But I think he often lies!"

"Oh, no!" cried the Old Past Master. "He doesn't lie. Masonry doesn't make liars of men! But a man can tell something that isn't true without prevaricating about it, you know. You don't know? Oh, well, you are young.

"You worked pretty hard today, didn't you? Of course. You always do, don't you? I thought I saw you over at the City Club this noon. Yes, I know that gang of chaps; fine fellows gather there every day for a couple of hours. Then you went up to the gymnasium, didn't you, and exercised for an hour? And you read the paper this morning before you went at your desk? That accounts for about four hours out of eight, but you'd swear you 'worked very hard'! You don't mean to lie; you just forget, or disremember, or are so used to calling that a hard day's work you don't realize what an easy time you have!

"'Tis the same way with the man who tells where he first became convinced he was to be a Mason! He means it, but he doesn't know or realize the facts.

"Now, I've been a Mason for many, many years. I have seen men come and go and hope to, some more. And I'll tell you that most men do not seek Masonry 'because they have conceived a regard for the institution' or 'because they wish to benefit their fellowmen.' Most men become Masons because other men whom they know are Masons, or because their fathers were Masons, or because they believe that Masonry means a certain patent of worth, or because they are curious, or even because they believe a Masonic membership will help them succeed.

"But those are not worthy motives," cried the Very New Mason.

"Perhaps not!" smiled the Old Past Master. "But we all do things from motives which are not worthy. You bought your wife a pair of theater tickets tonight and patted yourself on the back for being generous. Yet you know if you send her off to the theater with a friend she won't have a word to say about your coming home late from lodge! Do you call that a worthy motive? I call it a natural one, but St. Peter hasn't made a very large mark against your generosity score for the act!

"Now it would be glorious if all men wanted to be Masons because of the wonderful reputation which Masonry has among men. But if they did, Masonry wouldn't have nearly so much to do. And many men who become Masons for unworthy motives, remain to be taught to become very good Masons, indeed. I remember when I was twenty-one years old – bank clerk, I was – my boss said to me, 'Charlie, wasn't your father a Mason?' I said 'yes.' 'Your father rose very rapidly in this business,' said the boss. That's all. So I applied for the Degrees. I didn't know it wasn't a worthy motive! I knew it as soon as became a Mason. And all my life I have wished I had had a better motive. But I didn't let my ignorance stop me from trying to be a good Mason.

"Many very good Masons take certain parts of Masonry more seriously than they are intended to be taken. They are the chaps who think a misplaced word in the ritual is an anathema and the forgetter a criminal! They will tell you that any man who applies for Masonry for any other reason than a reverent awe for the Order and a humble belief in its wonder also commits a crime and should be excluded. It would be fine if it were so, but we'd have about one candidate a year if we held to any such interpretation of the law.

"If I find a young fellow who wants to be a Mason because his father was, I say, 'Come on in and welcome home!' That's supposing he is otherwise all right of course. If I find a young fellow who says very frankly, 'I believe it will help me in business,' I don't condemn him to be a profane forever. I try to find out what he means. If he wants to use Masonry to bring customers to his store, I tell him to go and think it over and come back in a year. But if he says, 'Why, all the Masons are clean-cut, honest men and I need to know such men and a lot of them, that I, too, can be clean-cut and honest, and it must help any man to succeed to be associated with clean-cut and honest men, and I want to succeed so I can bring up my boys to be good men too,' I can't see but that he is first-class material, supposing he's all right otherwise, of course.

"Look for the heart, boy, look for the heart! It's what's in the heart that counts, not what's on the lips. And that in my opinion, is what that question really means. 'Where were you prepared to be a Mason?' means, what sort of feeling have you in your heart? If it's a good feeling, I don't care how you analyze it; he who has it is welcome. If it's a bad feeling, then I don't care what fine words he mouths, it's enough to keep him away. I have known more than one man who joined through curiosity and yet became an ardent Mason. I have known more than one man who slipped in to aid him in business, became Master of his lodge and be a good one, too! Usually that man is the most insistent that all candidates have what he calls 'a clean mind' about becoming a Mason! The man who has had a change of heart after he gets in is always the most insistent on the statutory answer to the question as to where the candidate is first prepared to be a Mason! To me it is both funny and a little pathetic.

"My young brother, human nature is pretty much the same everywhere. Men are men in country and city, hamlet and metropolis. Most men make good Masons. A few make fine ones. Still fewer make poor Masons. Most men have quite human, ordinary, everyday reasons for wanting to be Masons. A few have fine reasons, a few have bad reasons. If the majority of men have just ordinary motives for becoming Masons, and yet the majority of men make good Masons, it's proof, isn't it, that Masonry is stronger than the motive, and it can change a man to her standards?

"I've lived a long time and the longer I live the more sure I am of the fertility of the soil in almost all good men's hearts, to the Masonic seed, and so I don't care nearly so much now, as I did forty years or so ago, why they want to be of us or where they were first prepared!

"Toleration, my brother, is a Masonic virtue. You'll feel that way too, when you've worn the apron as long as I have, and found, every year, as it grows closer to your heart, its strings of ritual and law and custom need bind less tightly."

The Ideal Mason

"So you think Brother Parkes is an ideal Mason, do you?" asked the Old Past Master of the Young Brother. "I like Brother Parkes, but before I gave assent to your adjective of 'ideal' I'd like to have you define it."

"What I meant," answered the Younger Brother, "was that he is so well rounded a Mason. He is Brotherly, charitable, loves a good speech and a good time, and does his Masonic duty as he sees it."

"Oh! Well, if that's being an ideal Mason, Parkes is surely one. But I can't follow your definition of ideal. For there are so many ideals in Freemasonry, and it has been given to few… I doubt, really, if it has been given to any… man to realize them all. Certainly I never knew one.

"There are so many kinds of Masons! I do not refer now to the various bodies a brother may join; Chapter, Council, Commandery, Scottish Rite Lodge, Chapter, Council, Consistory, Shrine, Grotto, Tall Cedars, Eastern Star; a man may belong to them all and still be just one kind of Mason.

"When I speak of 'kinds' of Masons I mean 'kinds of ideals'.

"There is the man whose ideal of Masonry is ritual. He believes in the ritual as the backbone of the fraternity. Not to be letter perfect in a degree is an actual pain to him; he cares more for the absolute accuracy of the lessons than the meaning in them. His ideal is a necessary one, and to him we are indebted for our Schools of Instruction, for our accuracy in handing down to those who come after us, the secret work, and to a large extent, for what small difficulties we put in the way of a candidate, by which he conceives a regard for the Order. What is too easily obtained is of small value. Making a new Mason learn by rote some difficult ritual not only teaches him the essential lessons, but makes him respect that which he gets by making it difficult.

"There is a brother with the social ideal of Masonry. To him the Order is first a benevolent institution, one which dispenses charity, supports homes, looks after the sick, buries the dead, and, occasionally, stages a 'ladies night' or a 'free feed' or an 'entertainment'. He is a man who thinks more of the lessons of brotherly love than the language in which they are taught; as a ritualist, he uses synonyms all the time, to the great distress of the ritually minded Mason. To the social ideal of Masonry and those to whom it makes its greatest appeal we are indebted for much of the public approbation of our Order, since in its social contacts it is seen of the world.

"There are brethren to whom the historical, perhaps I should say the archeological ideal, is the one of greatest appeal. They are the learned men; the men who dig in libraries, read the books, who write the papers on history and antiquity. To them we are indebted for the real, though not yet fully told story of the Craft. They have taken from us the old apocryphal tales of the origin of the Order and set Truth in their places; they have uncovered a far more wonderful story than those ancient ones which romanticists told. They have given us the right to venerate our age and vitality; before they came we had only fables to live by. To them we owe Lodges of Research, histories, commentaries, the great books of Masonry and much of the interpretation of our mysteries.

"Then there is the symbolist. His ideal is found in the esoteric teachings of Freemasonry. He is not content with the bare outline of the meaning of our symbols found in our lectures – he has dug and delved and learned, until he has uncovered so great a wealth of philosophical, religious and fraternal lessons in our symbols as would amaze the Masons who lived before the symbolist began his work.

"To him we are indebted for such a wealth of beauty as has made the Craft lovely in the eyes of men who otherwise would find in it only 'another organization.' To him we are indebted for the greatest reasons for its life, its vitality. For the symbolist has pointed the way to the inner, spiritual truths of Freemasonry and made it blossoms like the rose in the hearts of men who seek, they know not what, and find, that which is too great for them to comprehend.

"These are but other ideals of Freemasonry, my son, but these are enough to illustrate my point. Brother Parkes follows the social ideal of Freemasonry, and follows it well. He is a good man, a good Mason, in every sense of the word. But he is not an 'ideal' Mason. An 'ideal' Mason would have to live up to, to love, to understand, to practice, all the ideals of Freemasonry. And I submit, it cannot be done.

"What's your ideal of Freemasonry?" asked the Younger Mason curiously, as the Old Past Master paused.

"The one from which all the things spring", was the smiling answer. "I am not possessed of a good enough memory to be a fine ritualist; I don't have time enough to spare for many of the social activities of Masonry, I am not learned enough to be historian or antiquary, nor with enough vision to be an interpreter of symbols for any man but myself. My ideal is the simple one we try to teach to all, and which, if we live up to it, encompasses all the rest; the Fatherhood of God, and the brotherhood of man."

"Failure"

"What's troubling you?" asked the Old Past Master of a serious-faced brother who sat down next to him.

"So much I hardly know where to begin to tell it," came the response. "I try to be an optimist, but I can't help feeling that, practically speaking, Masonry is a failure, and it depresses me horribly, because I love it."

"Now that's too bad," said the Old Past Master soberly. "Masonry is a failure, practically speaking! That would depress me, too, because I also love it. In fact, I should think it would depress a great many men."

"Yes it would... a lot of men love it," said the troubled brother.

"Suppose you explain why it is practically speaking a failure," said the Old Past Master. "If I ought to be depressed because of such a condition I think I ought to know it."

The troubled brother looked up suspiciously, but the grave face in front of him wore no smile. If the old eyes twinkled they were hidden by solemn lids from the penetrating glance of the troubled brother.

"Well, it's this way," he began. "Masonry teaches brotherhood. Naturally, your brother is a man on whom you can depend; he is worthy of trust. One believes in one's brother. One backs his note and expects to be paid; one is willing to trust one's wife, one's life, one's good name, to a real brother.

"But there are a good many men who are Masons that I know are not worthy of my trust, merely because they are Masons. They are my brethren because I have sworn with them the same obligations and professed the same faith. But I do not think I could trust them with that which is of value to me, and I know they wouldn't trust me with what is of value to them. I don't mean they are not good men, but I don't feel that my Masonic bond is strong enough to give me the complete trust which a real brotherhood should provide and I don't think they feel it either.

"If I were in a strange city and a man came up to me and wanted to borrow two dollars and pointed to a Masonic pin as the reason, I wouldn't lend it to him. And if I walked into a strange bank and tried to cash a check for twenty dollars on the strength of my Masonic pin, I wouldn't get it."

"A pin, you know," put in the Old Past Master, "is not real evidence of being a Mason!"

"No, but even if I could convince the banker I really was a Mason he wouldn't cash my check without identification. And I wouldn't give money to a stranger even if I knew he was a Mason, because…well, because my brotherhood hasn't struck deep enough, I guess. And so it seems to me that practically speaking, Masonry is a failure."

"And yet you say you love it!" sorrowed the Old Past Master. My brother, you have, in the language of the street, got hold of the wrong dog.

"Now let me talk a minute. Your blood brother is a man you love. You were children together, you fought with him and for him. You shared his joys and sorrows. You learned him, through and through. If you love him and trust him, it is not because of your mutual parentage, but because of your association. Two boys are not blood brothers, but raised as brothers, may have the same tender love and trust. It isn't the brotherhood of the flesh, but the brotherhood of spirit, that makes for love and trust.

"You complain because you don't have that feeling for a stranger. Had you been parted from your blood brother at birth, and never seen nor heard of him until he met you on the street and demanded money while offering proof of his blood relationship, would you trust him without knowing the manner of man he had come to be? Merely because he was a blood relative wouldn't mean he was the type of man you are. He might have become anything during these years of separation.

"Now, my brother, when you became a Mason you assumed a tie of brotherhood with all the other Masons of the world. But you did not assume any obligation to make that tie of brotherhood take the place of all the virtues which are in the Masons of the world, or the virtues possessed by the profane. If you are a true Mason you will extend Masonic brotherhood, practically, to those Masons who hold out the brotherly hand to you; which means those men who are able and willing to prove themselves brothers and Masons, not merely those who belong to lodges and wear pins.

"The world is one big compromise, my brother, between things as they are and things as we would like to have them. You would like to be rich, and you compromise by getting what you can. You would like to be famous, and you compromise by being as well known as you can and doing the best you can to deserve fame. You would like to be the most highly skilled man in your profession, but you have to compromise with perfection on the one hand, and the need of earning a living on the other. As a Mason, you would like to trust on sight every Mason in the world, but you have to compromise with this fact that all Masons are human beings first and Masons afterwards, and human beings are frail and imperfect.

"Masonry makes no man perfect. It merely holds out one road by which a man may travel towards the goal of spiritual perfection more easily and with more help than by other roads. It had no motive power to drive men over that road; but it smooths the way and points the path. The travel is strictly up to the individual brother.

"If you trust those whom you know travel that path, they will trust you…and Masonry will be, practically speaking, for you both a success. If you travel with your eyes open, you will see many who fall by the wayside, not because the way is plain and smooth, but because they are too weak to travel it. That is the fault, not of the road, but of the traveler.

"And so, my brother, Masonry cannot be a failure, because men fail as Masons. As well say the church is a failure because an evil man goes to it; as well call Christ a failure because all men are not Christians. The failure is in the man, not in the beautiful philosophy which is Masonry."

"And I," said the troubled brother, "Am a failure now because I have failed to understand. But not in the future, thanks to you."

That "Atheist!"

"I am much troubled. A very good friend of mine asked me for a petition to this lodge, but when I took him one to sign he refused to do so, on the ground that he couldn't answer the question as to his belief in God."

"Well, I don't see that that's anything to be troubled about," answered the Old Past Master. "What he believes is his business, isn't it?"

"Yes, but —"

"But you want him in the Order," smiled the Old Past Master. "Well, it's not hopeless, my son. A lot of men say they don't believe in God, and mean something else entirely."

"How can a man say he doesn't believe in God and mean something else?" asked the Young Mason.

"What they usually mean is that they don't believe in the particular kind of God some one else believes in!" chuckled the Old Past Master. "I sometimes think such men are born just to give the angels something to smile about. Personally, I never found any necessity of defining God. But there are people who think they must measure Him with an idea, and fix a definite concept of Him in their mind before they dare say they believe in Him."

"But my friend," interrupted the Young Mason, "says he doesn't believe in any God, or Great First Cause, or Cosmic Urge, or Life Principle, or anything. He discusses it very well and seems unalterably fixed in his ideas. Yet he is a good man."

"Oh, yes, that's very possible," answered the Old Past Master. "Lots of very good men are very egotistical and conceited and —"

"But he isn't egotistical — why, he is very modest."

"There I differ with you. Any man who attempts to argue God out of the universe is certainly an egotist."

"But he doesn't argue Him out of existence; he just denies He exists."

"My friend," said the Old Past Master, "my little grandson tries to argue with me that the end of the rainbow is over on Park Avenue, and won't understand why daddy don't let him go and find it. He often explains to me how near the moon is, and I dare say he'd laugh if I told him the earth was round. He'd be perfectly sure we'd fall off the underside. He is only five, you know. Well, your friend is mentally only five.

"Have you ever read any thoughts of the great men on atheism? They are rather hard to controvert, some of them. Coleridge said, 'How did the atheist get his idea of that God whom he denies?' A clever Frenchman said, 'The very impossibility in which I find myself to prove that God is not, discloses to me His existence.' Bacon said, 'They that deny God destroy a man's nobility; for certainly man is like the beasts in his body, and if he not like God in his spirit, he is an ignoble creature.'

"No, my friend I very much doubt that your friend's atheism is real. It is a pose. He doesn't know it; doubtless he thinks to himself as very courageous, standing up and denying Him out loud. The very fact that it takes courage shows that the 'brave man' believes his statement outrages Something, Somewhere, Which may call him to account. What your friend probably means is that he doesn't believe in a God who sits on a cloud surrounded by a lot of angels playing harps, or that he doesn't believe in a God with a book in front of Him, saying to souls as they arrive, 'You go over there with the angels, but you get out of here and go to hell.'

"Yet both of these are perfectly good ideas of Deity, which satisfy a lot of people. There are millions and millions of people alive today who believe that God is called Allah. There are others who worship their Deity under the name of Buddha. To some God is a God of wrath, a stern God, a just God, but a God who may be appeased by sacrifice, pleased by song, distressed by sin. Man sees God in his mind according to his lights. The God one man believes in does not fit in with another man's ideas. And when he hears too many other ideas and likes none of them, he often says, 'I do not believe in God.' What he really means is, 'I cannot think clearly enough to visualize any conception of God which will do with what I know. I can't stand for the visions others have; therefore, I can't believe in any God,' never realizing that the very fact that he reasons about God, thinks about God, denies God, is very good proof of what he, nor no other man can get away from – the existence of God. Voltaire says, 'If God did not exist it would be necessary to invent Him.' Man can no more get along without God in his mind and heart than he can without air."

"Well, you don't think I should persuade my friend, do you?"

"Oh, certainly not. Masonry wants only those who know their belief well enough to state their faith in a Supreme Architect. Those other unfortunates who haven't struggled up through their own conceit and ignorance enough to understand their own belief in Some One, Somewhere – call Him what Name you will – must wait for the blessings of Masonry, even as my little grandson must wait until he is older before he can chase and capture the end of the rainbow.

"I do not argue that you should persuade your friend. I only tell you not to be distressed."

"But I am distressed as to what will happen to him. Won't God punish him for his atheism?"

"It is not for me to say what He will do," was the reverent answer. "But I do not think I should want to punish my little grandson for not believing me when I told him the end of the rainbow was not on earth, or for believing that the moon is near and can be reached with a ladder. I know he is but a little child and will learn better as his eyes grow clearer and his brain develops. Perhaps He thinks of us as just little children, and understands even when some deny Him."

"Where did you learn all this? Is there a book?" asked the Young Mason.

"I learned it from Masonry, my friend; what I have said is Masonry. Yes, there is a book."

"Can I get it?" asked the Young Mason eagerly.

"You can find a copy on the Altar," was the smiling reply.

Order of DeMolay

"It is going to be a very interesting meeting," said the Young Mason, sitting down in the anteroom beside the Old Past Master.

"I am glad you look forward with pleasure to it," came the ready answer, "but what especial feature intrigues you tonight?"

"Why, Brother Smith is going to ask for an appropriation from the lodge to help the Scottish Rite start a chapter of DeMolay. And there are a lot of the brethren who are going to object. You know, Sir, there are many of us who think that Masonry doesn't need any juvenile branches. And there are others who say the lodge should not give to a boy's organization, because many of the members have no boys but do have girls. So I expect there will be a warm discussion."

"I am glad you told me," said the Old Past Master. "It isn't often I get on my feet in the lodge anymore; I believe in letting the line officers run the lodge and in keeping old Past Masters where they belong on the side line. But now and then I get the urge to get up and talk, and this is one of those times."

"I am glad you are going to object to the appropriation," said the Young Mason. "That's the way I feel about it."

"I am not going to object," answered the Old Past Master, sharply. "I am going to urge the appropriation with all the force I have. I am going to puncture the feeble arguments of those who refer to DeMolay as 'Juvenile Masonry' and I am going to annihilate that brother who says he doesn't want lodge money spent for such Orders because he has daughters instead of sons."

"Why… why, you surprise me," cried the Young Mason. "Has it been drawn to your attention the DeMolay degrees are highly elaborate, spectacular and beautiful? Don't you think that a young man who sees such work will, when he becomes a Mason, be disappointed?"

"My young friend," answered the Old Past Master, "most of us live in small houses, in small towns, or bigger houses in big cities. Most of us do not live beneath the thunder of Niagara, or in site of the Grand Canyon, or in the shadow of Pike's Peak. Few of us live in or near Yellowstone, or the Yosemite, or Crater Lake. The larger part of the population of this country does not live in sight of the mighty ocean. Do you think it makes us dissatisfied with our lives and our homes that we go sightseeing among the beauties of this wonderful land of ours?

"I have seen the DeMolay degrees. They are much better put on by the boys, than our Masonic degrees are put on by the men. Is that the fault of the boys, their Order, their degrees, or is it our fault? Their degrees are beautiful and solemn; but that they even touch the skirts of the inner beauty of the Masonic degree, no real student of Masonry would admit for a moment. It may, indeed, be true that some young man, having taken the DeMolay degrees, will be disappointed when he gets his Third Degree in Masonry, that it is not more wrapped up in costumes, trappings, stage work. But such a young man would be disappointed in any event.

"I believe that most boys, when they grow up to be men, will turn from the elaborate and spectacular degrees of the DeMolay Order to the more quiet, thoughtful and deeper degrees of Masonry with relief, and will throw themselves in them with greater enthusiasm, because of their training in lodge room etiquette, their experience of fraternalism, their education in ritual and brotherhood.

"There are Masons in this lodge who will, I know, object to our spending money from the lodge treasury. They will say, 'why, I have no son to enter such an order, why should I help support it?' But they may have daughters. Then they are interested in having the young men in this town grow up to be good men, true men, square men. For some one of these young men, is some day, probably to be a husband to that Mason's daughter. And the better man he is, the happier she will be.

"Did you ever stop to think, my brother, what it is in Masonry which has kept it alive and made it grow, for thousands of years? What other thing can you name which has lived and grown for thousands of years? Only one, love and worship of God. Then I am speaking true words when I say it is the God in Masonry which has held it together. The Fatherhood of God and the brotherhood of man as taught in Masonry, are the inner cements which we spread with our trowels of degrees and lodges and ritual.

"The Order for the boys is but a new way of making ready the stones for our building. Before there was such an Order, we took young men as we found them. We still so take them. But in addition, we have now an Order which, while it speaks no word which can be construed as an invitation, which say nothing to any boy which would make him think Masonry wanted anything of him, yet teaches him patriotism, love of country, love of public schools, love of Masonry, because of its unity, its charity, its brotherhood, and teaches him too, the lessons of help to a brother, of broadminded tolerance and of sincere worship of a Supreme Being. No boy who has been a DeMolay will ever join a Masonic lodge without being better prepared to become a good Mason than the same boy would have been had he not been a DeMolay.

"There, my brother, now you know how I feel about it, and why I am going to urge that our lodge stand not in the way obstructing, but along side and pushing, that our young men have this glorious chance to learn the elements of fraternity before they come to us to be made Master Masons."

"And I am going to stand at your side and urge the same course," said the Young Brother. "I didn't understand."

For Love – Or Money?

I'm afraid we are not going to have the pleasure of hearing Professor Filson," said the Yearling Mason to the Old Past Master, sitting beside him in the anteroom.

"That's too bad," was the prompt response. "I don't know him. But I understand he's worth hearing. What's the trouble?"

"Oh, it's money, of course. Filson always gets a hundred dollars a lecture, and the lodge can't afford to pay it. And of course Filson can't afford to lower his price, and there you are."

"Why doesn't Filson give the Lodge the lecture then for nothing?" asked the Old Past Master.

"Why, why should he? That isn't business. The electric light company doesn't give us light, the printer charges us for printed matter, the furniture store charges us for carpets; why should Filson present us with his ware?"

"Seems to me there is a difference," suggested the Old Past Master. "Brother Filson, I suppose, comes to the lodge to spend an evening at times. When he does, he spends as much time here without paying, sitting on the bench, as if he were standing up talking. The electric light company could not give us current without spending money to produce it, the printer must pay his printers, the furniture man must buy his carpet. But Brother Filson would not have to spend any money to give his lecture; all he would have to spend would be a small part of what we have spent on him."

"I don't think I understand that last – what we have spent on him?"

"Thousands of years, millions of thoughts, untold effort, careful planning," was the prompt response.

"Listen, my son," went on the Old Past Master; "have you ever stopped to think just what Masonry is and does? Masonry is the product of the most unselfish thinking, the most whole-hearted and selfless effort, the world has ever known. Through it a universal brotherhood of millions of men has been brought into being, to any one of which you and I and Brother Filson have the right to turn, sure of sympathy, understanding and some help in time of need.

"Through Masonry, a system of philosophy has been evolved, and through its lodges that philosophy is taught to all brethren of the third degree, without money and without price. Through it we learn charity, toleration, courage, fortitude, justice, truth, brotherly love, relief. Through it we learn, decency, patriotism, high-thinking, honor, honesty and helpfulness. Through it, and all of these, we are made into better men, better citizens, better husbands, better fathers, better lovers, better legislators, better followers of our several vocations.

"Masonry may penetrate only a fraction of an inch beneath the skin of her followers, but by that fraction of an inch the man who takes even a little of her blessings to himself is a better man, and so the world is a better place for the rest of us. In some of us it strikes in deep, deep. We become soaked through and through with Masonic ideas, and strive, in our feeble, human way, to show forth to the world whatever measure we may accomplish of the perfection for which Masonry strives. Those of us who take it seriously and who love it much also make the world a better place for the rest of us.

"The lodge provides a spiritual home for brethren who may have no other. If one has another in his church, the lodge gives him a second spiritual home to which he may go once in a while and feel even more strongly, perhaps, than in his church, the close touch of his brother's hand, the sweet smile of a brother's love, the supporting arm of a brother's strength. To me, my lodge is a rest, a haven, a harbor for a tired mind. When I come to this lodge, whose destinies I guided so long ago, and which I have watched grow from a fledgling little body to a mature organization, I find myself uplifted, strengthened, made whole again. I may come tired, worn, weary with the day; I leave refreshed, invigorated, helped with the reviving of old truths, the remaking of old vows, the renewing of old ties.

"Our ancient brethren had 'cities of refuge,' to which the fleeing man, criminal or oppressed, might run for safety. Masonry is our modern 'city of refuge,' to which we, criminal in intent if we are such, or oppressed with injustice and cruelty, may fly for spiritual comfort and safety, knowing that within the four walls of a lodge is rest and peace and comfort.

"All this has the lodge in particular and Masonry in general, offered since the beginning, to all upon whom Masonry lays her gentle hands. You are the recipient of her bounty, as am I. And so is Brother Filson. We three – and all within these walls – take generously and without stint from Masonry's storehouse of loveliness, of beauty, of rest, and comfort and love.

"Often I ask myself 'what have I done for Masonry, which does so much for me?' Never do I feel that I have done enough. And Brother Filson, whom I do not know, might well ask himself that, before he thinks of what he might do for the lodge in terms of dollars, and prices and business. If, indeed, he has done one-tenth for Masonry and the lodge, what lodge and Masonry has done for him, he may hesitate. But if he is like the great, great majority of Masons, content to take much and to give little, willing to receive all and give nothing, careless of the structure which millions have raised in the past that he might benefit, unable to understand that to his hands, too, is committed the torch that those who come after may see clearly, he has need of open eyes, and an understanding heart, which alone may show him that for Masonry, which does so much for men, no man may do enough."

The Old Past Master ceased and sat silent. From a chair across the anteroom a brother rose and came slowly forward.

"I do thank you, my brother," he said, "from the bottom of my heart. The Lodge will certainly hear that lecture as soon as the Master wishes it. My name is Filson."

The Charity Fund

"I've been going over the lodge records," said the Yearling Brother to the Old Past Master in the corner, "and I am plumb discouraged."

"Why, the lodge records ought not to discourage you," smiled the Old Past Master. "Seems to me we have a right nice lodge record; books all straight, money in the bank, charity fund growing, and everything."

"That's the trouble...charity fund growing," answered the Yearling Brother. "It doesn't seem to me we do enough to justify ourselves or our existence. We have one brother in the Home. We are putting one young man through school, and we are buying three widows coal and paying one girl's bills out west so she can recover from threatened tuberculosis. And that's all. And we are a great big lodge."

"Well, wait a minute," said the Old Past Master. "When you say 'all' you mean all the big things. Of course, we spend some money all the time for immediate relief..."

"Of course," agreed the Yearling Brother. "But it seems to me we ought to do more big things."

"Such as putting a few more brethren in the Home?" smiled the Old Past Master.

"Well, of course, we can't put a man in the Home who doesn't need or want to go there," answered the Yearling Brother.

"How about buying some coal for your family, then?"

"Me? Why, man, I am no object for charity..."

"Well, do you know any brother of this lodge, or any relative of any brother of this lodge, who needs coal?"

"Er...no, I don't. But there must be such. We ought to take care of them."

"Well, why don't you go and hunt them up!"

"How can I hunt them up?" defended the Yearling Brother. "If they don't tell me, how would I know?"

"Exactly. And if they don't tell the lodge they need coal the possibilities are they don't need it."

"Now let me clarify your mind a little. You evidently have the impression, which so many people have, that the Masonic order is founded and conducted entirely for charity, for relief and assistance. Nothing could be further from the truth. Masonry is not an organization conducted for charitable purposes. It is not a mutual benefit association. Men are not permitted to join a lodge with the idea that they can get help from it. There are several very good Orders, whose insurance and relief and benefits are the principle things to be considered. A man who wants that sort of insurance should join one of them. But Masonry is devoted to teaching, not to helping with material aid. True, we do help; for we practice, as we teach, brotherhood. But we are not an organization for that purpose.

"If you have a blood brother, you don't expect to support him. You don't expect him to regard his blood relationship as a reason why he should sponge on you. You don't expect him to be continually asking for charity. If he has hard luck, or gets sick or is down and out, you put your shoulder to his wheel and push for the two of you. So do Masonic brethren, when one of their own gets in a hard case. But Masonry can choose her brethren, which the blood brother cannot do. Consequently, we aim to take into the order only men who will be pushers and not pushees.

"You think we ought to do more than we do. I tell you we are doing all there is to do. We are an upright, self-respecting, self-supporting lot. We have a fine membership. We have picked and chosen wisely. Only a few of us have fallen by the wayside. Those few we do our whole duty by. The reason we don't do more is that there is no more to do. The reason the charity fund grows is because we are wise enough to get only those members who won't need to use it."

"But," demanded the Yearling Brother. "If you carry the argument to its logical conclusion, the best lodge would be the lodge which had no indigents, and the charity fund of which would have no need for existence."

"Surely, the best lodge is the lodge with the best membership, of course. But if it has no need to use charity among its own members, there are always ways to use the funds for others. We contribute our share to the Home, for instance, whether we have a guest there or not. And we will forever, and when Brother Wells dies, we will be paying our pro rata for the brethren of other lodges, just as they now pay something towards our brother.

"The great objective of Masonry is to teach. It teaches good men to become better men. It teaches the Fatherhood of God and the brotherhood of man. It teaches the need of knowledge and the need of virtue. It teaches men to circumscribe their passions. It teaches toleration and uprightness and character. Its great end is to make men better men, and thus the world a better place in which to live. If we did nothing but charity, if all its efforts and all its funds went to charity, these great ends could not be so well accomplished. Masonry is charitable and its hand is behind all the fallen brethren, but it tries to pick brethren who will not fall, knowing that the more men who stand on their own feet, the more there will be to help those who do stumble, and the better it can teach its great lessons.

"Don't get off on the wrong foot, brother. This lodge does all it should do, all it can do, all it ought to do. No real appeal for help ever went unheard within its doors. And our resources would be behind that charity fund if it needed it. But thank the Great Architect, that we don't need to do more, that enough men in this lodge have learned the lesson of life as well as of Masonry, are discriminating in the selection of brethren who will help the lodge teach, rather than those who will help it become but a refuge of those who want help."

"What I need," confessed the Yearling Brother, "is someone to talk sense to me."

"What you need," countered the Old Past Master, "is experience; and a few years in Masonry. Time will give you both."

Masonic Libraries

"I can't just see the idea in founding this new Masonic library," objected a comparatively newly made Master Mason, talking to a group in the anteroom during refreshment. "Books are all right, of course, and libraries are necessary, but why insist on such a complete library for the new Temple?"

"Well, why not?" asked someone.

"If you follow out the idea to its logical conclusion," answered the new Master Mason, "the Elks ought to have a library and the Knights of Pythias ought to have one. The I.O.O.F. should support a library and the Red Men should have one, too. All the hundred and one fraternities should have libraries and the curious spectacle would be presented of a hundred groups of a few hundred men each, each supporting its own little collection of books. Wouldn't it be much more sensible if they all supported one big collection?"

There was a moment's silence. The group turned questioning eyes to the Old Past Master.

"We already support one big collection of books," the Old Past Master began. "All of us here present contribute our quota towards the support of the city library. In practically every town of any size in the nation is a local library, which all support by their proportion of taxes.

"But the general library for the general run of people is naturally general in character. It will have books on science and history and travel and adventure and mathematics and botany and business and poetry and art... a great many books on a great many subjects, but no authoritative collection on any one subject. The doctor may use the library for general purposes, but when he wants the last word, he goes to his medical library. The lawyer may use the general library for one purpose or another, but it is either his personal law library or that of his Bar Association which he depends upon for accurate information in regard to a knotty point of law.

"A Masonic library may partake of the character of a general library, in that it may have a lot of fiction and current literature. It serves Masons in that way, just as the coffee and sandwich at refreshment serves him. The Lodge isn't and doesn't pretend to be, a restaurant, but it gives him something to eat to make his visit pleasant. The Masonic library isn't, and doesn't pretend to be, a competitor of the city library, but it gives him some fiction and some current literature to serve him at his pleasure."

"But the main purpose of a rightly conducted Masonic library is to convey knowledge to its owners and users. Masonry makes much of the liberal arts and sciences; not to provide the means by which Masons may learn of these is for Masonry to fail in practicing what she teaches.

"The Masonic library is poorly conceived and ill furnished which contains only books upon Masonry. A doctor's library which had books only upon office practice and business systems would be of little help to the physician. The Masonic library which has only Masonic history and philosophy, offers but little to the true seeker of light. A Masonic library should be a library of all knowledge, including a great deal on Masonry, but as much on philosophy, science, religion, art, history, that its users have the opportunity to learn.

"In the capital of this nation is America's largest and finest collection of books; the Congressional Library, second only to the library of the British Museum in size, and with its volumes far more accessible to readers than that of the English library. But that doesn't prevent the Ancient and Accepted Scottish Rite for the Southern Jurisdiction from maintaining one of the very finest Masonic libraries in the world. In the great House of the Temple are a hundred thousand books. They are not all books on Masonry, though the Masonic collection is world famous. It is a general library, of general knowledge. Incidentally it contains a wonderful Burnsiana collection, the largest collection of English translations of Goethe's Faust in the world, as well as the priceless Pike manuscripts, some of them not yet in print.

"Yet in spite of this there is a Grand Lodge library in the capital of the nation, for the use of Master Masons, and the local Scottish rite bodies got up a library of their own, by asking members for unwanted books.

"I think every Order should have its own library. I see no reason why Elks and Red Men, Pythians and Odd Fellows, should not find equal benefits from libraries of their own. But there is this distinction; Masonry is old, old. It is worldwide. Its history is the history of the world. Its philosophy is the philosophy of all ages. With not the slightest disrespect for the various other fraternal orders, it may truthfully be said that none of them has the lineage, the extent, the spread, the history or the intimate connection with knowledge that is Masonic pride. Therefore, Masonry has, perhaps, an especial need for books, and books, of course, mean a library.

"Something has been said about including books in lighter vein in Masonic libraries. I think they should be included. One gives candy to a child to make the taking of medicine easy. We supply entertainment and refreshment to make attendance at specially vital meetings, easy. Why not the inclusion of books of purely entertainment character to make the use of the library easy to those who know little of libraries? As those who once came to scoff remained to pray, so it is often the case that the man who starts browsing in a library after light fiction remains to examine, and be interested by, works of real information.

"So, my brethren, I believe we should support our Masonic library to the limit; I believe we should make sacrifices for it, help it, use it.

"Masonry has only gentle methods at her hand for the working out of her great purposes. We wield no battle- axe and carry no sword. But... the pen is mightier than the sword, and the book is but the printed thought which some man penned. Education is Masonry's greatest tool; and books are at once the foundation and the superstructure of education."

"I wish I could learn to think first and talk afterwards," said the newly made Master Mason. "I am for all the help we can give."

"You see," smiled the Old Past Master, "even talking about a library has help our brother's education."

The Masonry You Make

"Well, I know you'll be glad to hear I am through learning the Work!" announced a young brother to the Old Past Master, "One more lesson and I'll know all about Masonry!"

"That's fine, son. I congratulate you!" answered the Old Past Master.

"Some conceit!" murmured another brother, as the satisfied young brother moved away. "I've been studying Masonry many years and I don't think I know all about it, by a long chalk!"

"Of course you don't, and neither does he. But we all have to learn of the Masonry we make for ourselves."

"Oh, do you think so? I thought we learned of the Masonry our ancient brethren had made for us!"

"That, too, of course. But the Masonry they made for us is the Masonry which can be written down, or put in symbols, or taught by word of mouth. It is a concrete thing; a thing of words and phrases, of symbols and figures, of stone and wood and temple and rough ashlar and square and compasses. But the inner Masonry... that we make for ourselves.

"Do you ever read Ingersoll? Somewhere he says 'an honest God is the noblest work of man' and thousands of people have shuddered away from the sentence and call it blasphemy. But they fail to understand what the great agnostic meant. Our modern conception of the Great Architect of course falls infinitely short of reality, but at least we do not do him the injustice of confining Him within the limits of our human frailties. But up through the ages man has limited his gods and his God, according to himself. The gods of Greece and Rome (to go no further back) were gods and goddesses who felt jealousy, anger, revenge. They interfered in the affairs of men for their own pleasures. They were made in the image of men who made them! Later, God was a cruel tyrant, who sanctioned the torments of the Inquisition and loved those who were wicked in his name... at least, such was the middle ages' conception of Deity. Only within a few hundred years has the world as a whole come to consider God as the all-wise, all-loving, all-merciful, all-tender Father of us all. This was what Ingersoll meant when he spoke of the honest God as the noblest work of men; and honest conception of a God infinitely wonderful and beautiful, is a noble conception.

"Masonry is a conception. After one gets through learning the ritual, the mere words and phrases, he begins to absorb the philosophy and moral system of Masonry. Still later he begins to carry Masonry in his daily life and live by it. Later on... but wait a minute. We have word Masons to whom the ritual is the whole. We have Masons to whom the symbolism is the whole thing, and who see nothing beyond the inner meanings to squares and compasses and stones and angles. We have others who add to this, philosophy of Masonry, but to whom Masonry is yet a perfect system which can be learned in its entirety by those who apply themselves.

"But there are others... more every year, thank God!... who make their own Masonry, beyond that of the books and the lodge, the word and the symbol. To these, Ingersoll might have said that 'an honest Masonry is the noblest work of the Craft' with no more irreverence than he intended in his famous epigram.

"Masonry, to such thinking men, is illimitable. It has no end. It is as infinite as space, as unending as time, as distant in boundary as the faintest nebula. It is not a thing of earth only; it encompasses the universe, and joins man's hands with God. This is the Masonry we make for ourselves, and, could what we make be measured, its proportions would be exactly the proportions which are our own. For the hidden Masonry we make is large or small, wide or cramped, beautiful or ugly, grave or gay, useful or ornamental, fine or doss, exactly as are we.

"In each of us is an idea conception of all we would attain. We have our ideal man, our ideal woman, our ideal job, our ideal position, our ideal happiness. Some of us are so inarticulate we cannot express them; some of us are so inchoate in our thinking we cannot clearly visualize them, but they are there, these ideals, each and every one a measure of what we are.

"And we have, also our ideal of Masonry, the hidden Masonry we make, each man for himself. Your inner temple is not like mine and mine is not like yours, though each may be beautiful and perfect; two faces may be equally lovely, you know, yet totally unlike.

"To my way of thinking, we are better Masons as we grow our inner Masonry for ourselves, as we perfect it and polish it, and raise it higher and higher. It is sadly true that no man may teach another how to build this hidden temple, but it is beautifully true that all of us may build the better by getting for ourselves better working tools. And the working tools with which we as Craftsmen build our own inner, hidden temple of Masonry, into which none may ever step but ourselves and God; the rough and perfect ashlar, square and plumb, trowel and compasses, by which we build this edifice, are available for us all. Our young friend has one, when he secures a perfect working knowledge of the ritual. The student has another, when he has mastered most of the symbolism. The doctor has a third, when he understands and can formulate the philosophy of Masonry, and all of us get a new edge to our tools as we live according to Masonic light and gain in Masonic experience."

The Old Past Master stopped and looked off, as if he saw a vision.

The brother to whom he spoke sighed. "I wish," he said, "I might have the inspiration of looking at your temple of Masonry, that I might make mine better."

When Laughter is Sad

"Oh, it's going to be rich. The poor fish is scared to death. And you know when Abbot does the work in the third degree how, er… well, let's call it impressive, he is."

The Young Mason chuckled at the thought.

"That's not going to be the only funny thing happen Wednesday night," answered another newly raised brother. "I happen to know my friend Ted is going to do the Senior Deacon's part. And Ted gets stage fright. He doesn't lose his memory or anything, but his voice goes up about an octave and a half; oh, it's funny. I laughed, last time I heard him…"

"I had a good laugh at one of the members of my class when I went in," chimed a third voice. "He couldn't understand what was going on and objected to every move and generally reminded me of a bucking billy goat. I laughed until I cried. I shall look forward to Wednesday night…"

"I wonder," broke in a quiet voice, "if you young gentlemen realize what it is you are saying?"

"Why… why… why of course, we do. We haven't said anything wrong, have we?" inquired the first speaker of the Old Past Master sitting quietly in the corner of the anteroom, listening.

"I am an old, old man," countered the Old Past Master, gently. "I have lived a long, long time, and the longer I live the less able I am to classify anything as wholly right or wholly wrong. I wouldn't say that in what you said is wrong in the sense that it is intentional evil. It is wholly wrong from my point of view, to bite the hand that feeds you, to abuse hospitality, to belittle the agency that helps you, to deride and make sport of holy things, to injure that which is valuable to others even though valueless to yourself."

"But, good heavens, man. We haven't done any of those things. Why, I only said that Abbot is so impressive he'd make a good laugh come out on Wednesday's degree…"

"That was enough, my brother. Is there a church into which you would go with the idea of laughing at a penitent at the Altar? Is there a church in which you would think it right to laugh at a communicant partaking of the bread and wine? Is there a church where the spectacle of a man on his knees would make you laugh, no matter how odd or peculiar he was or how he was dressed?"

"Of course not. I don't laugh in church…"

"Then why laugh in the lodge? In all the third degree, is there humor? Do you not know that it is a tragedy which the third degree portrays, a tragedy no less that it teaches an inspiring lesson, and has the inspiration of all that is good and noblest in a good man's character?

"What do you think a candidate thinks when the most solemn, the most sacred, the most secret of a Master Mason's lessons is being given to him, if from you, and you, and you on the benches, comes smothered laughter? Will it add anything to the impressiveness of the degree in his eyes? Will he feel that what he is being given is sacred, valuable, precious to his heart? Or will he say to himself, 'Evidently there is a catch in this somewhere… I guess it's a joke, and I am it!'

"You have spoken of Filby, who has stage fright and whose voice raises an octave because of it. Filby wasn't blessed by nature with a beautiful voice, but God gave him something precious to Masonry, and that is earnest, sincere, genuine enthusiasm. I have been in this lodge for more years than you have been on earth, and I have never known a Senior Deacon to put more into his work than Filby does, though he has a poor voice. The words Filby uses are inspired words; the degree he puts on is a noble degree. And Filby does it as if inspired by its nobility. Would you laugh at a hero saving a life because he was dressed in caps and bells? Can't you hear, beyond poor Filby's cracked vocal chords, the chimes pealing in his heart as he tries to make his words impressive and beautiful?

"Another of you has found it funny when a candidate for the third degree has not understood his part and made it difficult for the team to put him through the ceremony. At Receiving Hospital last week they brought in a young man suffering from a broken arm. He was very ignorant; one of those foreigners who understands little or nothing of American ideas and ideals. And to him a hospital was a torture place, a house where doctors cut people to pieces for their pleasure. He was frightened almost to death and struggled and fought, while the surgeons tried to control him that they might set his arm. Was it funny? Or was it sad, that ignorant people had so destroyed his faith in his kind that he couldn't recognize kindness and help when he saw it?

"The man who was too frightened to understand and so made his third degree difficult was a victim of those who had tormented an imaginative mind with the idea of goats and pain and indignity in a Masonic lodge. I find nothing funny in it; only sadness.

"Don't think of me as an old kill-joy. A good laugh at some wit in a business meeting, a good laugh at a good story after lodge; these are all well and good; wholesome and natural. Whether they are located in a lodge, a church or a home, they are good.

"But not in a church during service, not in a lodge during a degree. There is no laugh in the lodge during any degree which is not an insult to the officers, and a badge of ignorance and ill manners for him who laughs. Charity we can preach; charity we should practice towards those who do not do so well in the degrees as we think we might; the fraternity is not to be laughed at because there are some who make one part of the third degree less real than strenuous.

"Look, my brother, for what lies beneath; regard not so much the outward form as the inward meaning and you will not again be tempted to consider a degree as a substitute for a vaudeville performance, a lodge as a temple of laughter."

The Old Past Master ceased and sat quiet, waiting.

"But I say!" cried the Young Mason, "Don't you think you are a little rough with us?"

"You are all much too good material to allow to spoil for the sake of your feelings," answered the Old Past Master with a smile.

"But you sure take a chance we'll dislike you for plain speaking."

"What do I matter? You may dislike me… but I don't believe you will laugh in lodge again!"

"I'll say I won't either!" answered the Young Mason. It's a promise… and I'd like to shake hands!"

A Mason's Christmas

"I don't believe in a Christmas celebration by the lodge. I don't think we ought to have one, or be asked to contribute to one or in any way engage in Christmas festivities."

"The Junior Mason spoke emphatically and with marked disapproval of the little ante-room group nearby, making happy plans for Yule-tide.

"That's very interesting," commented the Old Past Master. I like to hear points of view unfamiliar to me. Would you mind telling me why?"

"Of course not. It's very simple. Masonry is not Christian. King Solomon, of course, wasn't a Christian, nor were either of the Hiram's. Masonry admits to her ranks any good man of faith; Christian, Jewish, Mohammedan, Buddhist… it makes no difference, so he has a Faith. Then, as a lodge, we celebrate a holiday belonging to one faith. Now I personally am a Christian, and of course I celebrate Christmas. But my brother across the way is a Jew, who does not recognize Christianity. To ask him to spend his proportion of lodge funds in celebrating the birth of a Leader in Whom he does not believe would be exactly like asking me to celebrate, with my proportion of lodge money, the birth of Confucius. Of course, I have only one vote and the majority rules, but when it comes to personal contributions to a Masonic Christmas celebration, my hands will never come out of my pockets."

He shoved them deeper in as he spoke to emphasize his intention not to spend.

"Hm!" answered the Old Past Master. "So you think your Jewish brother across the way doesn't recognize Christianity? Don't you mean he doesn't recognize Christ as the Son of God?

Wait a minute… Oh, Brother Samuels." The Old Past Master called across the anteroom. "Here a minute, will you?"

The Jewish brother rose and came forward.

"I just wanted to ask you if you are in favor or against the lodge Christmas celebration?" asked the Old Past Master.

"Me? I am in favor of it, of course, both for the lodge appropriation and the individual contribution."

"Thank you," nodded the Old Past Master. Then as the Jewish brother went back to his seat, he turned to the Junior Mason.

"You see, my son, our Jewish friend is not narrow. He does not believe in Christ as the Redeemer, but he recognizes that he lives in a country largely Christian, and belongs to a lodge largely Christian. To him the Christmas celebration is not one of His birthday, but of the spirit of joyousness and love which we mean when we sing, at Christmas time 'Peace on earth, good will towards men!' If you argue that 'peace' is only a Christian word, he might even quote to you the words of One who said 'I bring you not Peace, but a Sword.'

"Now let me explain something to you. The Jew has just as much right to refuse to recognize Christ as the Son of God, as you have to refuse to consider Mohammed the Prophet the followers of Allah say he is. But as an educated man, you must know that Mohammed was a good man, a devout leader, a wise teacher. As an educated man, you admit that the religion founded by Buddha has much in it that is good, and you admit that Confucius was a wise and just leader. Were you in the land where the birthdays of any of these were celebrated, would you refuse your part in the people's joy in their Leader, simply because you followed another? I trust not. Well, neither do our Jewish brethren or our Mohammedan brethren, desire to be left out of our celebration. They may not believe in the Divinity of Him we, as Christians, follow, but if they are good men and good Masons… they are perfectly willing to admit that the religion we follow is as good for us as theirs is for them, and to join with us in celebrating the day which is to us the glad day of all the year.

"Believe me, boy, Christmas doesn't mean Christ's birthday to many a man who calls himself Christian. It is not because of joy the He was born that many a good man celebrates Christmas. It is because his neighbor celebrates it, because it is a time of joy for little ones, because it is a day when he can express his thanks to his God that he is allowed to have a wife and family and children and friends and a lodge, because of that very 'peace on earth' spirit which is no more the property of the Gentile than the Jew, the Chinese or the Mohammedan.

"It is such a spirit that Masons join, all, in celebrating Christmas. It is on the Masonic side of the tree we dance, not the Christian side. When this lodge erects its Christmas tree in the basement and throws it open to the little ones of the poor of this town, you will find children of all kinds there; black, white, yellow, and brown, Jew and Gentile, Christian and Mohammedan. And you will find a Jew at the door, and among the biggest subscriptions will be those from some Jewish brethren, and there is a Jew who rents cars for a living who will supply us a dozen free to take baskets to those who cannot come. And when the Jewish Orphan Asylum has its fair, in the Spring, you will find many a Christian Mason attending to spend his money and help along the cause dear to his Jewish brethren, never remembering that they are of a different faith. That, my son, is Masonry."

"For Charity is neither Christian nor Jewish, nor Chinese nor Buddhistic. And celebrations which create joy in little hearts and feed the hungry and make the poor think that Masons do not forget the lessons in lodge, are not Christian alone, though they be held at Christmas, and are not for Christians alone, though the celebration be in His honor. Recall the ritual: 'By the exercise of brotherly love we are taught to regard the whole human species as one family, the high and low, the rich and poor, who, as created by one Almighty Parent, and inhabitants of the same planet, are to aid, support and protect each other'.

"It is with this thought that we, as Masons, celebrate Christmas, to bring joy to our brethren and their little ones, and truly observe the brotherhood of man and the Fatherhood of God, whether we be Jew or Gentile, Mohammedan or Buddhist."

The Old Past Master ceased and stood musing, his old eyes looking back along a long line of lodge Christmas trees about which eager little faces danced. Then he turned to the Junior Mason.

"Well," he said smiling, "Do you understand?"

"I thank you for my Christmas present," came the answer. "Please tell me to which brother I should make my Christmas contribution?"

Understanding

"I have been a Mason for a year now," remarked the Young Brother to the Old Past Master "and while I find a great deal in Masonry to enjoy, and like the fellows and all that, I am more or less in the dark as to what good Masonry really is in the world. I don't mean that I can't appreciate its charity, or its fellowship, but it seems to me that I don't get much out of it; I can't really see why it has any function outside of that relationship we enjoy in the lodge room and the little charitable acts we do."

"I think I could win an argument about you," smiled the Old Past Master.

"An argument about me?"

"Yes. You say you have been a Master Mason for a year. I think I could prove to the satisfaction of a jury of your peers who would not need to be Master Masons; that while you are a lodge member in good standing; you are not a Master Mason."

"I don't think I quite understand," puzzled the Young Mason. "I was quite surely initiated, passed and was raised. I have my certificate and my good standing card. I attend lodge regularly. I do what work I am assigned. If that isn't being a Master Mason, what is?"

"You have the body but not the spirit," retorted the Old Past Master. "You eat the husks and disregard the kernel. You know the ritual and fail to understand its meaning. You carry the documents but for you they attest but an empty form. You do not understand the first underlying principle which makes Masonry the great force that she is. And yet, in spite of it, you enjoy her blessings... which is one of her miracles, that a man may love and profit by what he does not comprehend."

"Why... I... I just don't understand you at all. I am sure I am a good Mason..."

"No man is a good Mason who thinks the fraternity has no function beyond pleasant association in the lodge, and charity. Man, there are thousands of Masons who never see the inside of a lodge and therefore, perforce, miss the fellowship. There are thousands who never need her charity and so come never in contact with one of its many features. Yet these may take freely and largely from the treasure house which is Masonry.

"Masonry, my young friend, is an opportunity. It gives a man a chance to do and to be, among the world of men, something he otherwise could not attain. No man kneels at the Altar of Masonry and rises again the same man. At the Altar something is taken from him never to return; his feelings of living for himself alone. Be he never so selfish, never so self-centered, never so much an individualist, at the Altar he leaves behind him some of the dross of his purely profane make-up.

"No man kneels at the Altar of Masonry and rises the same man, because, in the place where the dross and selfish was, is put a little of the most Divine spark which men may see. Where was the self-interest is put an interest in others. Where was the egotism is put love for one's fellow man.

"You say that the 'fraternity has no function.' Man, the fraternity performs the greatest function of any institution at work among men, in that it provides a common meeting ground where all of us, be our creed, our social position, our wealth, our ideas, our station in life what they may, may meet and understand one another.

"What was the downfall of Rome? Class hatred. What caused the Civil war? Failure of one people to understand another, and an inequality of men which this country could not endure. What caused the Great War? Class hatred. What is the greatest leveler of class in the world? Masonry. Where is the only place in which a capitalist and laborer, socialist and democrat, fundamentalist and modernist, Jew and Gentile, gentle and simple alike meet and forget their differences? In a Masonic lodge, boy, through the influence of Masonry… Masonry, which opens her portals to men because they are men, not because they are wealthy or wise or foolish or great or small but because they seek the brotherhood which only she can give.

"Masonry has no function? Why, son, the function of charity, great as it is, is the least of the things Masonry does; the fellowship in the lodge room, beautiful as it is, is at best not much more than one can get in any good club, association, organization. These are the beauties of Masonry, but they are also beauties of other organizations. The great fundamental beauty of Masonry is all her own. She, and only she, stretches a kindly and loving hand around the world, uniting millions in a bond too strong for breaking. Time has demonstrated that Masonry is too strong for war; too strong for hate, too strong for jealousy and fear; the worst of men have used the strongest of means and have but pushed Masonry to one side for the moment; not all their efforts have broken her, or ever will!

"Masonry gives us all a chance to do and to be; to do a little, however humble the part, in making the world better; to be a little larger, a little fuller in our lives, a little nearer to the G.A.O.T.U. And unless a man understands this, and believe it, and take it to his heart and live it in his daily life, and strive to show it forth to others in his every act; unless he live and love and labor in his Masonry, I say he is no Master Mason; aye, though he belong to all Rites and carry all cards, though he be hung as a Christmas tree with jewels and pins, though he be an officer in all bodies. But the man who has it in his heart, and sees in Masonry the chance to be in reality what he has sworn he would be, a brother to his fellow Masons, is a Master Mason though he be raised but tonight, belongs to no organization but his Blue Lodge and be too poor to buy and wear a single pin."

The Young Brother, looking down, unfastened the emblem from his coat label and handed it to the Old Past Master.

"Of course, you are right," he said, lowly. "Here is my pin. Don't give it back to me until you think I am worthy to wear it."

The Old Past Master smiled. "I think you would better put it back now," he answered gently. "None are more fit to wear the square and compass than those who know themselves unworthy, for they are those who strive to be real Masons."

Carl H. Claudy

The Better Way

"See that young chap over there? Yes, with the red hair and the glasses! Had quite a time with him this evening! He is red-headed inside as well as out, and he loves Masonry so much he wants to fight for her all the time!

"What was his trouble? Oh, he wanted to prefer charges against a brother and have a Masonic trial and purge the fraternity of a rascal and be a sort of combination Sir Galahad, Joan of Arc and Carrie Nation to this lodge.

"It seems he has some inside information about some brother of this lodge who has done several things a Mason ought not to do. Sold some goods by misrepresentation, worked his women employees longer than the law allow and threatened to fire them if they told, kited a check or two and was warned by the bank... I really don't know all his high crimes and misdemeanors!

"But it's all fixed now. Red head is calmed down. There will be no preferring of charges just yet!

"Glad of it! I should say I am glad of it. Don't get the idea in your head that preferring charges and holding a Masonic trial are matters to be joyful about! At times... sad times they are... it is necessary to do it. But there are many more times when it could be done, but it is far, far wiser not to do it.

"I had to agree with him, of course, that our erring brother was no ornament to the lodge, if what was said of him was true. I admitted freely that a man like that should never have been permitted to be a Mason. But I couldn't see that throwing him out would do the fraternity any good and it would certainly not do him any good. And it would do us a great deal of harm, both as a lodge and individually.

"You don't see why? Well, let me tell you. Ever since Cain wanted to know whether he was his brother's keeper, men have

57

felt that they were their brother's keepers. And so, indeed, we should be. But 'keeper' doesn't mean prosecutor. When you 'keep' your brother, you keep him from harm, you keep him from evil, you keep him from danger. You do not throw him under the wheels, push him out into the cold, do him an injury. When you 'keep' your brother, it is the man, not his conscience, you keep.

"The Jesuits showed the world what keeping as man's conscience for him might do; it resulted in the inquisition. Masonry has no business following in such footsteps. We do not, and should not, try to keep our brother's conscience. We should, indeed, aid him, help him; we should try to show him the right if he is wrong, we should, indeed, 'in the most friendly manner, remind him of his faults.' But it is a far cry from this to holding a trial and kicking him out.

"When is a Masonic trial right? Well, to my mind, only when a man has done something which, unregarded and unpunished by his lodge, will hurt Masonry more than the scandal of getting rid of him will hurt it. Now this brother has not as yet been disgraced in society. He has not been arrested, tried or convicted. He may, or may not be guilty of those things with which the red head charges him. It is good American doctrine to believe a man innocent until he is proved otherwise, and Masons are good Americans. For the lodge to take the initiative in a trial for offence against a civil law would be both unMasonic and unwise.

"Leave him alone? Certainly not. He won't be left alone. This man has friends in this lodge. Red head is getting them together and laying his 'facts' if they are facts, before them. Those friends can be trusted to see that the man is told of the talk which is going on, and given a chance to explain, to deny, to affirm, to mend his ways if they need mending. Obviously, we don't want as a brother in the lodge a man who continuously violates the common tenets of all humanity, but equally as obviously, we don't want to accuse and stigmatize a man as doing so, unless we know we are right.

"Every man knows that a man unjustly accused before the law and acquitted is never wholly cleared from the taint. There are always some who say 'yes he was accused and got off. But they took him to court,' as if it was a disgrace. The man who is tried by Masonry for an offense, and acquitted must always be, to his brethren a man about whom scandal was whispered. There are always those who say 'no smoke without some fire.' So we don't want to prefer charges and have a trial unless we are pretty sure of what we know and equally sure of what we want to do. It is much better for any lodge to have one bad egg in its omelette, than to spoil the whole omelette. One bad egg in a ten-egg omelette will spoil it, but in a five hundred-egg omelette it isn't so noticeable. It is much better for us to go quietly after this brother and try to get him to do better, to appeal to his manliness, his Masonry, his friendship, than it is to insist on a Masonic trial.

"No, my brother, there are better ways. The charges preferred, the Masonic trial, the disgrace, the scandal, the hard feelings are very bad for a lodge, very hard on those who take part, very severe on the one who is either acquitted or held guilty. Never, until all other means have been tried and found unsuccessful, should they be used; never then, until several wise heads have been consulted. When the time comes, when there is no other course open, then may charges be preferred and a trial held, and the lodge purged of that evil element which is harming it. But we must be very sure that the remedy isn't worse than the disease, and that in scotching the snake we are not also fatally injuring the hand which scotches.

"Red head listened to reason; his friends and those of a brother who may be at fault will do the rest and the good old lodge will never be hurt. And under all, and over all, we will have the happy knowledge that we are practicing that toleration and charity of thought which makes us our brother's keeper in the best, not the worst sense of the word."

"Silk Stockings"

"Well, what do you know about that!" exclaimed the Young Mason, as a dress-suited figure with a jewel on his coat stepped in front of the Altar. "That's Jamison, Past Master of Joppa-Henderson Lodge."

"I see it is," answered the Old Past Master. "But what is it that surprises you?"

"Why, that anyone from Joppa-Henderson should leave the sacred confines of his own lodge and come to a simple, democratic, every-day lodge like this one, let alone a Past Master. I never could get this 'silk- stocking' Masonic idea, anyhow. Of course, you know, they have two hundred dollar fees and forty dollar dues and you can't get in unless you have a bank account, an automobile, a wife with diamonds and a box at the opera."

"Is it as bad as all that?" asked the Old Past Master, smiling. "You didn't, by any chance, make application to Joppa-Henderson and get refused, did you?"

"I certainly did not. And I would not, under any circumstances. Why, you know it isn't Masonic. Here in this lodge- look along those benches. There is Branch, who lays bricks for a living, and Taggert, who is a bookkeeper, and sitting next to him is Wilson, who is a bank president, and there is Colton, street car conductor, and Dr. Baird, the X-ray specialist, and Hillyard, who sells ribbons down in the department store, and Ellsworth, who is a Senator – democratic, this lodge is! Here you find real Masonry. We really do not regard any man for his worldly distinctions here – but in Joppa-Henderson Lodge –"

"Have you ever heard of a man being refused in Joppa-Henderson because he isn't wealthy?" asked the Old Past Master.

"Certainly not! They never apply there," was the scornful answer.

"Ah! Now we are getting at the meat of the matter. My brother, you could travel about a bit to your advantage. You will find, if you look, there are many different kinds of lodges. For instance, in the metropolis is a French lodge; that is, almost entirely composed of Frenchmen, who are Americans, not French Masons. You wouldn't want to join that lodge, and perhaps they would rather you wouldn't. Yet it is a fine lodge of fine men. There is a Daylight Lodge in the city which meets in the afternoon. Its membership is almost wholly among theatrical and newspaper men who cannot meet at night. You wouldn't feel at home among them, perhaps, and yet they are good Masons. There are several lodges in this country composed almost wholly of Masonic students; you wouldn't feel at home with them, but that doesn't mean they are not good men and good Masons. And while it is true that the members of Joppa-Henderson Lodge are almost wholly well-to-do business and professional men, it happens so because the lodge was founded by fifty such, who naturally attracted to each other their own kind.

"If, indeed, what I may call a class lodge refuses an application because he doesn't belong to that class, that lodge is unMasonic. But I don't think it works that way. I think the class lodge attracts its own kind of people. I would call this a class lodge. It is a very democratic organization, with an intense pride in what you have just noted; that is, mixes all kinds of men in the Masonic cauldron and thus cooks a truly Masonic brew. You are attracted to this lodge for that reason, and so were the men you named. But men who are essentially aristocrats may not feel as much at home among the democrats as among their own kind; for such there is Joppa-Henderson Lodge.

"The ideal system of Masonry considers all men are alike and all lodges are alike, just as an ideal democracy is founded on the theory that all men are free and equal. This country is a republic, with democratic ideals, yet we all know that we are not all equal, and no words will make us so. The bricklayer isn't the financial equal of the banker, and the banker isn't the labor equal of the bricklayer. But don't get the idea that because two things are unequal, therefore one is better than the other. A circle and a triangle are not equal, but is one better than the other?

"Joppa-Henderson, and all so-called 'silk-stocking' lodges, newspaper lodges, class lodges of any kind, are not equal to each other; they are quite different. But that does not mean that one is any better or any worse than the other. And each attracts its own kind of men, to whom it gives a precious Masonic light, they all do their work. Without some of these class lodges, good men might not be attracted who now are; without Joppa-Henderson, for instance, we might not have visiting us tonight one of the finest Masons, most earnest Masonic workers and most brilliant Masonic officers this jurisdiction ever saw. So I say to you, my brother, beware how you judge the other fellow and his lodge, lest he, in turn misjudge you.

"I have known Joppa-Henderson Masons for years. I have visited their lodge many times. The way they do their work is an inspiration. And I have never known of a man rejected in that lodge that I couldn't guess why he was rejected; and it was never for anything else than his character. Money plays no part. They are as willing to take the hod-carrier or the chimney sweep as we, if he can live up to their schedule of finances. But the poor man isn't attracted to that lodge; he goes to a lodge where he finds the simple democracy we have here.

"All lodges who do honest and sincere work, my brother, have their places in the great system we call Masonry. There is room for all kinds; the high, the low, the rich, the poor, the democratic, the aristocratic. This lodge, with an income from dues of twenty-five hundred dollars last year, spend a few dollars more than a thousand for charity. Joppa- Henderson with an income from dues of sixteen thousand, spent ten thousand in charity. Charity is but one measuring stick, but by it, they measure up."

"Yet you," countered the Young Brother, "stick to this lodge, and don't demit to Joppa-Henderson."

"Perhaps I can do more real Masonic work here," smiled the Old Past Master, looking the younger brother full in the face.

The younger brother had the grace to blush.

The Pledge

"Haven't paid your pledge yet? Well, brother, it's not ethical for me to ask why. That's your business. What? Peeved at the Committee? Now, you do amaze me! How do you expect them to build the Temple if you, and twenty thousand like you, don't do what you promised to do? You think they shouldn't 'dun' you for the money? Well, they shouldn't have to! But human beings are prone to forget and put off, and the stone masons who build the Temple have to be paid, and their families have to be fed and they have to eat and they can't wait, I suppose, until you get over your peeve!

"There are a lot of brethren, you know, who make pledges to pay a certain amount towards the erection of a new Temple and then don't do it. You can't say they break their promise, because they truly intend to pay 'some day.' But they break the spirit of the promise when they don't pay when they have promised to pay. And they... and you, my brother... have taken an obligation which should prevent you from withholding even the value of a penny, knowingly, from your brother to whom you promised it.

"There are all sorts of reasons for not paying! There is your childish reason... being 'peeved!' Any one would think to look at you, that you were truly grown up. Yet you let a grievance against one brother, or one set of brethren on a committee, keep you from fulfilling your obligation to all your brethren in this jurisdiction. If you, as a parent, were peeved with the school board, would you keep your child from school? If you were peeved at the Mayor, would you refuse to allow the fire engines to put out a fire in your home? If you were cross with the boss of your ward would you refuse to let the policeman he had appointed, arrest the burglar trying to steal your goods and chattels? Probably not! Yet here you are, offended at the committee and saying to them, in effect 'because I don't like the way you act, I will refuse to put my stone in the Temple. For all of me, there can be a hole in the wall. Not that I have any grudge against my brethren, or any crossness with the fraternity or any ill-will to Masonry, but the only way I can get even with you, who offend me, is to make it difficult for you to serve my brethren!'

"Don't you think that's rather childish?

"Now, Brother Jones over there, he has another reason for not paying. He isn't peeved or anything, but he doesn't like the design of the Temple! He says 'you tear it down and build it up over again, and build it long where it is now short and short where it is now long. Put 17 pillars in it instead of seven, or 70, and I'll pay my hundred dollars' or whatever it is he has promised.

"Nice, reasonable human being, Jones! But he is logic itself compared to Smith! Smith doesn't pay because he says he has so many other things to pay and 'they won't miss my little pledge.' Imagine Smith, when he makes a note to the bank for his pay roll. Comes around another month and the note falls due. But Smith won't pay... not he! He goes to the bank and say 'I'm sorry, but I have to pay a lot of other things this month. Just tear up the note and forget it, won't you? I have changed my mind about paying the note!'

"What? Why yes, it is a parallel case, exactly. Smith gave his word to his brethren that he would pay a certain amount towards the new Temple. The Committee believed him, just as they believed the rest of the Masons who pledged their aid. And because they believed in a Mason's word, they obligated the fraternity to stone masons and electricians, to iron workers and plasterers, to builders and plumbers, to do the work. Just suppose every one of the pledgers refuse because they have other obligations? Where will we find the money to pay our debts? Is Masonry to stand discredited before the world because one brother has a childish peeve, another doesn't like the design of the Temple, a third finds it inconvenient?

"My brother, a pledge to pay money, on which other men act, should be as sacred as a secured obligation to a bank. The Temple is being built by Masons, for Masons. It is to be a testimonial to all the world that here is a seat of truth, of light, of freedom of thought, of reverence for God, of brotherly love, of comforting philosophy… of Masonry. If what we teach sinks into our hearts, there will be no unpaid pledges.

"Luckily for us all, the great, great majority of Masons do as they agree. They pay what they promise. They stand behind their word. That is how the Temple is built… how all Masonic Temples are built. That is how all temples of any kind are built, whether they be of stone, for Masons, or in the heart, for God.

"Most Masons mean what they say when they kneel before the altar and pledge their lives to brotherhood. They do so without any evasion in their minds or hearts. Most Masons when they pledge their money to a Masonic cause, pledge it without evasions on their mind or heart. Most men, thank God, are honest, and a very large number of honest men are honest Masons and… what are you doing? Oh, I see you have your checkbook and your fountain pen. I trust, my brother, that nothing I have said has offended you! I wouldn't make you mad with yourself because you haven't paid, for anything. All I tried to do was to transfer that peeve from the Committee to the chap who didn't play fair, but who, I see, is now going to play fair! Yes, I see; the check is for double your pledge. I think, if you take it over and show it to Jones and then to Smith, and tell them all I said, you will feel better and they will feel worse… why, certainly, my brother, I am proud to shake the hand of any of my brethren, especially when I find them as real underneath as you. What? Oh, don't mention it!"

Those Symbols

"I think I shall have to take an evening off and read a book about symbols!" said the Very New Master Mason to the Old Past Master at refreshment. "I find I don't know all about them."

"When you find the book which teaches you all about them, lend it to me, won't you?" asked the Old Past Master.

"Why, I'm sure there must be such a book," answered the Very Mew Master Mason, surprised. "And I know you know all about symbols, anyway."

"I have never read a book which even attempted to tell 'all about symbols,' " answered the Old Past Master. "I never knew the Mason who was willing to admit he knew all about them. And I never thought I knew very much about them, although I have studied them for forty years!"

"Why, you amaze me! There are only half a dozen symbols in the lodge; surely they cannot have so many meanings. The tools, the apron, I suppose the pillars on the porch; that's about all, isn't it?"

The Old Past Master turned and looked curiously at his questioner. Satisfied that he was serious, the Old Past Master explained, gently, as to a child.

"I doubt very much that any one has ever had the temerity even to count the Masonic symbols," he began. "Certainly I have not. But there are enough to keep a great many Masonic scholars and antiquarians busy for a great many years to come, as they have in past, trying to dig out of literature, history, archeology, sacred writings, religion, philosophy, and kindred branches of study, a few of the more important meanings of our symbols. Your innocent little catalog of lodge symbols would be pathetic if it wasn't funny, and humorous if it wasn't sad!

"Certainly you could not have meant to overlook the Great Light as a symbol, and…"

"Oh, but I don't understand that as a symbol," interrupted the Very New Master Mason. "That's the Bible, the Book. I thought a symbol was something that meant something else!"

"It is true that in our American and in British Lodges the Great Light is the Holy Scriptures," agreed the Old Past Master. "But in another lodge, in another country, some other sacred Book may lie on the altar. The important thing is not what book there lies open, but that it be the book which the Masons who kneel before it, venerate as the earthly repository of spiritual knowledge. Thus, to our Jewish brethren, the New Testament in our Great Light is not a Sacred writing as is their Old Testament. Yet our Book contains both.

"But the Book of the Law when used in Masonry is more than a repository of Divine Will and Knowledge. It is a symbol of the fountain head of all learning, and a symbol of a Mason's belief in Deity. It is also a symbol of many other things, of which you will find in the books you will read, but in none of them will you find it all.

"Did you ever stop to ask yourself why Masons circumambulate in the lodge? Or why they perform

this rite at various times and in various ways? Or why that rite in a Blue Lodge is always done in one direction? That is a symbol, my brother, and a very beautiful one. It is a connection, tenuous, but very direct, with those far progenitors of Masonry who lived thousands of years ago and worshipped the Sun as the only god they knew.

"It is human to be like those we strive to admire. The small boy plays at being a soldier or a fireman, and struts with a small cane to be like his father. Imitating, we feel that we are like that which we imitate. Our savage forefathers had this same bit of humanness. They believed that when they imitated that which was powerful, they in turn received power. They worshipped the Sun. The Sun, to them, travelled always from the East to the West, swinging north in the summer and south in the winter. Therefore they believed that if they, in their simple prayers and rites, imitated the course of the sun, they, too, would become godlike and have power. Many religions, rites and ceremonies of a spiritual significance have followed in the footsteps of these early men, and thought to find in circumambulation a power which comes from the Divine Something they worship.

"Of course there are other meanings of circumambulation; these, too, you will discover in the books you will read.

"Not all our symbols are so ancient, although some are even further back in time. You are familiar, of course, with the 'certain point within a circle.' That is a symbol and a great one. It has many meanings; meanings not attributed to it haphazard, but meanings born in it, as you might say. A Mason may not materially err if he circumscribe his passions within that circle, not because the ritual says so, but because our ancient brethren, who actually built Temples and Cathedrals, found that the point, or center in the circle, and another dot or two, were their easiest means of making their squares perfect, and absolutely at right angles. This is a little problem in geometry with which you are doubtless familiar; if not, the books you will read will explain it to you.

"Get out of your mind, my brother, the idea that any symbols in Masonry are arbitrary; that some man said, for instance 'here is an oblong square; I will make it into a symbol which means the lodge, just because I like the shape!'

"The 'oblong square' my brother, was the shape which our ancient brethren conceived the world to be. We use it as the 'shape of the lodge' because the lodge itself is a symbol of the world, and thus of our life in it.

"My brother, symbolism in general, and Masonic symbolism in particular, is a life-time study. It is ever new, never ending. The more you read and study, the more you understand and enjoy this Masonry of ours. But you will learn it not in one evening or two; not even in many shall you learn it all."

"Unless I spend them talking to you," smiled the Very New Master Mason.

Ancient Landmarks

"I bought me a Masonic Manual today," announced the Very New Master Mason to the Old Past Master. "Into what strange paths I am about to venture I don't know, but I am going to try..." rather shyly... "to learn some of the work."

"That is very commendable," agreed the Old Past Master. "You will find it a fascinating study."

"But there are a lot of things in it I don't understand," went on the Very New Master Mason. "For instance, in the charge to a Master Mason the Master says, 'the ancient landmarks of the order, committed to your care, you are carefully to preserve and never suffer them to be infringed' and so on. But nowhere can I find any explanation of just what the ancient landmarks are!"

"Well, that is a problem, isn't it?" smiled the Old Past Master. "If you will get Mackey's Jurisprudence you will find a list of twenty five, Roscoe Pound has a list of seven in his book of the same name, Brother Joseph Fort Newton considers five is the number and several Grand Lodges have lists up to fifty or sixty!"

"Do you mean to say there are no universally known and understood list of ancient landmarks?" demanded the Very New Master Mason.

"I do. There is no such list."

"But... but... but then how can we 'carefully preserve them' and 'never suffer them to be infringed?' "

"Well, it really isn't as difficult as it sounds!" smiled the Old Past Master. "There is none, or hardly any, disagreement among Masonic authorities on the fundamental Masonic law. The ancient usages and customs of the fraternity are the same the world over and generally recognized as such by all Grand Bodies. But a 'landmark' is something that cannot be changed, according to our understanding of it. Therefore, different authorities have thought differently about our ancient usages and customs, some saying that such and thus, while ancient and honorable, is not a landmark, and therefore can be changed, while others hold that the same custom is a landmark and cannot be changed.

"The old manuscripts which give us so much light on our Masonic forbears; the Regius, the Harleian; the Antiquity, etc., have various charges, rules, regulations and laws. These are all very old, yet many of them could hardly be considered a landmark; for instance, one such old regulation forbids Masons to indulge in games of chance except at Christmas! That would hardly do for a Masonic landmark, would it? So just because a rule or custom is old does not make it, per se, a landmark.

"On the other hand, much that is beautiful in our fraternity is new; that is, it is less than three and often less than two hundred years old. There was no Grand Lodge before 1717, and Masonry was not divided in three degrees at that time, I believe. Yet many authorities consider the division of the work into three degrees as a landmark.

"So where doctors disagree, only the patient can decide!"

"There are a certain body of laws, usages and customs which are universally recognized and regarded. From these, different authorities select certain ones which in their judgment are landmarks. Other authorities say 'no, thus and such is a law, statute, rule, judgment, agreement or custom of the fraternity but isn't a landmark!' Brother Shepard has just brought out a book on the subject which gives the ideas of many authorities, writers and Grand Lodges. What strikes me on reading it, is not the difference in the lists of what are called landmarks, but the fact that all so well agree as to what is fundamental in Masonry!

"Now it is a fact that we agree that the 'ancient landmarks' are fixed and unalterable. It is also a fact that Masons themselves have altered their own unalterable landmarks! The very fact that

Grand Lodges were invented, or discovered, or created, is a change in an old, old custom, made necessary by change in times and people. The issuing of diplomas was a change; for ancient brethren had only the 'Mason word' to prove themselves Master. We do not prepare a man to be made a Mason as was done two centuries ago, nor is our ritual the same, nor our obligation the same; antiquarians have even discovered where parts of our obligations came from, and it was not from a Masonic source that all of them were derived!

"But let not your heart be troubled! Masonry herself says of herself that she is a progressive science. How can she progress and stand still? Brother A. S. McBride than whom no more spiritually minded or common sense writer ever spread Masonry before the Craft for their better understanding, asks the literal-minded Mason who says nothing can be changed in Masonry, why not work in Hebrew, since Solomon and his workman used that tongue? And does Masonry suffer because the English of today is not the English of the 17th century?

"I personally believe that the ancient landmarks which cannot suffer change are few in number; a belief in Deity, a belief in a future life, a book of Law on the altar, a secret mode of recognition, that only men, of good character, can be made Masons; these and one or two more seems to me to be real landmarks. Other landmarks so prescribed seem to me… and to many deeper Masonic students… to be common law, custom, usage, rather than landmarks.

"But I only think these things. I do not try to convince any one I am right, for those who decide have authority and scholarship behind them. I follow where they lead. Bit Masonry teaches a man to think, and so I do her no injury if I do think. And if my Grand Lodge says forty-seven laws are landmarks, I keep them like Kipling's Mason 'to a hair.' That I choose to disagree with my Grand Lodge in my heart doesn't make me a law-breaker;

only a minority. And there is no harm in being a minority as long as one conforms!

"Therefore, read your manual, learn your ritual, consult your Grand Lodge records, and abide by the laws, resolutions and edicts you have sworn to uphold. And when you have done that, tolerant charitable Masonry says to you 'my brother, having done as you pledged you would, you may now think whatever you want is right!'"

Do You Study Geometry?

"I bought me a high school geometry the other day" confessed the Very New Mason to the Old Past Master, sitting on the benches waiting for the Worshipful Master to call the lodge to labor. "I was so much impressed with what I learned of its importance to Masons, during the Fellowcraft Degree, that I determined to go back to my school days and try again. But I am much discouraged."

"Why so?" asked the old Past Master, interested. "I recall geometry as rather an interesting subject. I don't suppose I could do a single original now, it's been so many years… I don't know when I have looked in one!"

"Why, you surprise me! I thought all good Masons must know geometry. We are taught… how does it go?… something about a noble science…" his voice trailed off in silence.

" 'Geometry, the first and noblest of the sciences,' " quoted the Old Past Master, " 'is the basis on which the superstructure of Masonry is erected. By geometry, we may curiously trace Nature through her various windings, to her most concealed recesses. By it we may discover the wisdom and the goodness of the Grand Artificer of the universe and view with delight the proportions which connect this vast machine.' "

"Yes, that's it!" agreed the Very New Mason. "And there is a lot more, isn't there?"

"A whole lot!" smiled the Old Past Master, in agreement.

"Well, then, why doesn't a well informed Mason have to be a geometrician?"

"There is certainly no reason why a good geometrician shouldn't be a good Mason," answered the Old Past Master, "but no reason why a man who doesn't know geometry shouldn't be a good Mason.

"You see, my son, we hark back a great many years in much of our lectures, to a time when knowledge was neither so great nor so diversified as now. William Preston, the eminent Masonic student, scholar, writer, who lived and wrote in the latter part of the eighteenth century, conceived the idea of making the degrees in general, and the Fellowcraft degree in particular, a liberal education! A 'liberal education' in those days was comprised within what we still call, after Preston, the 'seven liberal arts and sciences.' In those days any mathematics beyond geometry was only for the very, very few; indeed, mathematics were looked upon rather askance by the common men, as being of small use in the world, save for engineers and designers and measurers of land.

"But Preston, if his lectures are no longer the real 'liberal education' which he planned, and which, in the form of his lectures modified by Webb (and somewhat tinkered with by various authorities and near authorities who at times have kept the husk and let the kernel escape!) builded better than he knew. For we may now justly and honorable take 'geometry' to mean not only the science of measurement of surface and area and the calculation of angles and distances, but to mean all measurement. And to study measurement, my son, means to study science, for all science is but measurement, and by that measurement, the deduction of laws and the unraveling of the secrets of nature.

"I do not understand geometry anymore; it is long since I studied it. But I do study, and do try to keep my mind awake and always filling, if never full. It is true that to many a Mason the study of geometry itself would be a grand mental discipline and thus greatly improve his mind. But I do not think we are to take this admonition literally, any more than we are to accept literal interpretations for other wordings in our ritual. We meet upon the level, in Masonry, and we act upon the square. But that does not mean that we put our feet upon a carpenter's level, or sit upon stone masons' squares while we 'act.' The words are symbols of thoughts. I take the admonition to study geometry as a symbol of a thought, meaning that a Mason is to educate himself, to keep his mind open, to keep it active, to learn, to think, to develop his reason and his logic, the he may the better aid himself to know himself and his work to aid his fellowmen.

"Even Preston, literal-minded as he was, and focusing all his attention as he did, upon ritual and teaching by it and a formalism which is not yet outworn in our ranks, had a vision of what geometry might mean beside the mathematical science of angles. For… how does it go? In our charge to a Fellowcraft, we say, 'Geometry, or Masonry, originally synonymous terms, being of a divine and moral nature, is enriched with the most useful knowledge, while it proves the wonderful properties of nature, it demonstrates the more important truths of morality.'

"It should be obvious that a study of mathematics of any kind cannot demonstrate morality unless it is considered a symbol as well as a science. As we are thus told in so many words to use geometry as a symbol, we may well agree with Pike, who wrote learnedly to prove a Mason's inherent right to interpret the symbols of Freemasonry for himself. To me, geometry is a symbol of science, and one which I should use to impress upon myself the need of something else. To a Mason who had had few educational advantages, the word might mean its literal sense, and he be greatly benefitted by a close study of the book which discourages you.

"I do not attempt, my brother, to force upon you my understanding, or to quarrel at all with those Masons who find a different interpretation of the geometry which is Masonry as we understand it. I do but give you my ideas for whatever use they may be to you, and so you will not be discouraged in what is a praiseworthy attempt to profit by the Masonic lectures. Do you recall the end of the charge you received as a Fellowcraft?"

"I… I… I am afraid I don't, just exactly…"

"It runs this way," smiled the Old Past Master. " '…in your new character it is expected that you will conform to the principles of the Order by steadily persevering in the practice of every commendable virtue.' If you study the 'principles of the Order' you will, indeed, be learning Masonic geometry."

Work To Do

"I want some Masonic work to do!" announced the newly raised Master Mason. "I don't think I should be a member of this great fraternity and stand around idle."

"That is very praiseworthy," responded the Old Past Master. "What would you like to do?"

"Well, I don't know exactly. Maybe I could help in building a new Temple. Perhaps I could do some research work and write a book. Maybe there is room for me in some great Masonic educational work."

"You aim high," answered the Old Past Master. "Such work is not always easy to find."

"It's all I have been able to find," answered the first speaker.

"That is because your eyes are not yet opened to the light," answered the Old Past Master. "Masonic work is everywhere. It lies around loose ready to be done. You find it here in lodge, at home, on the street, everywhere."

"Oh, you mean charity. Well, I give according to my pocket-book," was the answer.

"I do mean charity, but not pocketbook charity," answered the Old Past Master. "Masonic charity neither begins nor ends with money."

"I wish you would explain what you mean. I don't understand…"

"I will very gladly explain. Do you see Brother Eggleston over there?"

"The old man with the ear-horn?"

"Exactly. He is eighty-two years of age. He is very hard of hearing. He is also extremely fond of being talked to. It's a hard job to tell him anything. You have to shout. Yet Brother Eggleston always has some one talking to him at refreshment and in the anteroom.

"Just behind him is Brother Palinski. He doesn't speak very good English. He isn't very rich. He is very shy. Yet he is a member of this lodge and a good one. Have you met his acquaintance? You need not answer. I am not inquiring what you have done, but just suggesting to you that he feels more at home and more Masonic when his brethren do not let him sit alone and unspoken to, because he is foreign, different, hard to talk to.

"Jimmy is the Tiler of this lodge. He works pretty hard, does Jimmy. You and I and a hundred other fellows take off our aprons and drop them where we sit when lodge is closed. Jimmy has to gather them up and fold them neatly in the box. Jimmy has charge of the clothing and the jewels and locks up the charter in the safe. Jimmy has to be here early and leaves late. He doesn't get paid very heavily for his work. Sometimes some brother stays and helps Jimmy do his work. Jimmy is always happy when he, too, can get out in time to hop into some one's car and get taken part way home.

"Do you run an automobile? Somewhere within half a mile of you live two or three or four old Masons who find walking hard and streetcars uncomfortable. They love their lodge, but they do not always come when it rains, because it is hard on their old bones to walk or take the trolley. Sometimes some brother thinks of them and calls for them and takes them home. The brother who does this rarely thinks he has done anything except afford transportation, but you have to be an old man and have a young one pay you a little attention to know how it makes their old hearts sing. I am an old man, and I know, although I have a car and a son to call for me, yet I like attention; I like to think some one doesn't think I am on the shelf. I like your asking me questions. I like to feel that I am some use to Masonry, even now.

"You give, you inform me, according to your pocketbook. You smoke I observe, very good cigars. At Roberts Avenue and Upshur Street is a children's hospital. In it are many little children. Some of them belong to Master Masons. Not all of their parents can get there every day, or bring a toy to while away a tedious hour every time they come. The price of two of those cigars would make a Mason's child happy for a week.

"Last month there died a Mason of this lodge, who left a wife and five children. He left plenty of insurance. His wife doesn't have to go to work. She can support herself and her children very easily. No lodge action was necessary. But what a place for Masonic work! Those children now have no Daddy. They have problems only Daddy could solve. No one can jump in and become a Daddy to them, but some Mason might try to ease that awful empty feeling, with his presence and his interest.

"Wilkins, of this lodge, works at the electrical trade. He makes things with his hands; anything, everything. But mostly he makes wireless sets; a little radio apparatus that isn't expensive, but is better than can be bought for a few dollars. He puts in most of his evenings making them. The lodge supplies the material. The little sets go to the State Home for the Blind. I wonder sometimes, if the little head pieces do not speak Masonic words to those who listen to them so gratefully.

"Do you know Filbert? Poor Filbert; it's an open secret. That's Filbert, over there with the young face and the snow white hair. He had an accident. It took a year for his strength to come back. His mind never was quite right, and isn't now. He loves to come to lodge. He isn't very bright, any more. He is just a watchman now, who used to be a bookkeeper. Filbert has an eighteen-year-old boy, putting himself through college. He has to work at odd times and nights and Sundays. He does everything he can; waits on table, cuts grass, runs errands, paints fences, anything. You might give him a job now and then; I think it would be regarded as work on your Master's Piece by the great Architect."

"Oh, I hope it would… but what you have done for me just now, I know is work on your Master's Piece!" stammered the young Mason. "Indeed, my eyes were not open, but I… I begin to see the light!"

Those Legends

"I am a very much disturbed person!"

The speaker, a newly made Master Mason, addressed the Old Past Master earnestly.

"I have always believed, as I always believe my Bible, that the story of Solomon's being our first Grand Master was true. I have always believed that Masonry has come down to us through the ages substantially as it is now. I have always believed in the reality of the drama of the third degree. Now I find that great scholars say it isn't so!"

"Poor boy!" soothed the Old Past Master. "He has discovered that his dolls are stuffed with sawdust. Some one took away his Santa Claus! Fairies have been banished from his heart and he grieves!"

"I didn't think you would make fun of me!" protested the Young Mason.

"My dear brother, I don't make fun of you! I speak with all seriousness!" protested the Old Past Master. "You are exactly in the position of your young child who is robbed of Santa, who learns that fairies do not exist, who finds that a doll is made of powdered wood. But, like a child, you will outgrow the grief. If you go to your wife's most secret hiding place in the attic, the chances are ten to one you will find and old and much-loved doll. She knows it is only sawdust, but she loves it. And I bet a cookie that you send Christmas cards to your friends and like to go and see some one dressed up as Santa, distributing presents at Christmas. As for fairies, did you, or did you not, enjoy reading and seeing Peter Pan? The grief is gone; the joy remains!"

"But what has that to do with Solomon and Masonry?"

"A whole lot!" answered the Old Past Master. "The greatest truths have been taught by parables and stories. It is the best way of teaching, for it touches the imagination. For instance, it is obviously a truth that a man should remember his parents in their need, take care of his children, and be charitable. The far Easterner puts it in a fable. A man going to the bazaar buys seven loaves of bread. 'For what do you purchase so many, Oh, Effendi?' asked the merchant. 'Two I return, two I lend, two I give, and one I use,' answers the buyer. 'Explain, Effendi,' begs the merchant. 'The two I return to my parents, who once gave to me. The two I lend are to my children, who will one day return to me. The two I give are for charity and the one I use is for myself.'

"Is not that a pretty way of teaching? And does it not make a far greater impression on your mind that the mere statement of fact?

"It is so with the Solomonic legend. We know that modern Freemasonry began little more than two hundred years ago. We trace well-defined ancestors of Masonry through the Roman Collegia, the Comacines, the Steinmetzen of Germany, the Compagnionage of France, the Guilds of medieval England. We find Masonic symbols in Egypt and ancient Babylon. We find Masonic philosophy in many lands in remote ages. There is no doubt that the forebears of our own Masonry were very far back in time, perhaps even further back than Solomon. That there is any direct connection between Solomon, the King of Israel, and a modern Grand Lodge cannot be established.

"But neither can we establish any connection between Christmas and Santa Claus! How shall you teach a small child of the beautiful spirit of Christmas by telling him it is to celebrate the birthday of Christ? You can't. He cannot comprehend. How may you teach a newly made Master Mason all the history of Masonry, all at once? You can't. In either case you require a legend. And make no mistakes about it, my friend; the facts of the legend may be all wrong. But the spirit of both legends is entirely true!

"Now Freemasonry is not concerned with facts; 'twice two is four' is far less interesting to Masonry than 'he gives twice who gives quickly.' Masonry is wholly a matter of the mind, heart, spirit, will, character, desire, love, veneration of us humans. It is not concerned with heating or lighting or invention or armies or haystacks. The spirits of the Solomonic and Hiramic legends are true; they are true to the heart, just as the Christmas myth is true to the child. You never saw a fairy, but your life would be the poorer without them! You never showed your little child a Santa Claus, but his life would be poorer without him. Masonry cannot show a direct, logical, provable, evidential descent from Solomon, but Masonry would be the poorer without the legend which teaches of her beautiful beginning in the erection of a Temple of God, and the wise guidance she had from the most learned man of all time.

"For, it is not the facts of our legends with which we are concerned, but what they teach. With the trowel we spread the cement of brotherly love. Did you ever feel, see, taste, smell, any of that cement? Did you ever see any one use a trowel to spread it? It is not true, in the fact sense, is it? Yet you believe it, I believe it, even when we know it is but an allegory, a symbol, a truth expressed in fiction.

"If the lesser lights be put out, can you see the Great Light? You cannot. The Great Light does not emit radiance for physical eyes. No one thinks it does. Yet its radiance makes Masonry.

"Trouble not your heart, my brother, that antiquarians have let in the light and discovered the facts. We are always the better for facts. But your very searcher after Masonic facts would be the first to defend the legends. Masonry is old, old; old as the human heart. Lodges, degrees, Grand Masters; these may, indeed, be young. But the principles of Masonry are ancient as the world, and if we teach them with allegories of words as well as of symbols, it is because that is the best way to teach any heart!

"Personally, Solomon is as real to me as my fairies and my Santa Claus, and you, nor any other man can rob me of their spirit by denying to me their letter!"

"Nor to me, either, and more!" answered he newly made brother.

When Twice Two Is Five

"Masonry is contradictory!" sighed the Young Master Mason at refreshment. "I am sure I will never get the right of it in my stupid head!"

"It is something to recognize that it is contradictory!" smiled the Old Past Master. "But just what particular contradictions are worrying you now?"

"Oh, a whole lot of them. For instance, we do not recognize negro Masons, yet I am told there is a lodge composed of negroes in this country, which is a part of, and works under, one of the regular, recognized State Grand Lodges. I read that there are women Freemasons abroad and yet we are taught that no woman can be a Freemason. I have just read the wonderful story of Roosevelt Lodge in Providence, R.I., and thus found out that there are lodges which refuse to admit foreigners and Jews; yet we teach and claim that Masonry is universal and without sect or creed. Kipling, in his Mother Lodge poem, has a Roman Catholic a member of it, yet everywhere I hear that Masons are opposed to Catholics. I am told in Lodge that there is no religion honored in Masonry, yet there is a Grand Lodge, I am informed, which bases itself and its teachings on Christianity!"

"Well, you are rather up against it!" smiled the Old Past Master. "Yet is really very simple. Let me ask you a few questions."

"Shoot! If questions will help me, I'm here to answer!"

"What do you regard as the most civilized nation on the face of the earth?"

"America, France, England, I don't know which."

"What is the abiding principle of Christianity?"

"Love."

"What is the fundamental of all foundations of this government of ours?"

"Freedom, liberty, I suppose."

"Is war civilized?"

"Certainly not! It is barbarous."

"Is murder a matter of love?"

"Gracious no! Matter of hate, I should say! What are you getting at, anyway?" asked the Young Master Mason.

"Can you think of any examples in our national life in which liberty is abridged, either within or without the law?"

"Plenty of them!"

"Well, then," explained the Old Past Master, "we have civilization which is contradictory, government which is contradictory and the greatest and most far reaching religion which the world has ever known, contradictory!"

"Oh, no!" cried the Young Master Mason. "Because we made war doesn't mean civilization is a failure; we failed civilization. Because murders are committed by Christians doesn't mean Christianity failed; the murderers failed. Because some people violate the laws of liberty doesn't mean our government fails; they fail."

"You are a bright scholar!" admitted the Old Past Master. "And because there are contradictions in Masonry it doesn't follow that Masonry is contradictory, but that Masons contradict each other! It is true that we do not recognize negro Masons, as a general rule. It is true there is a recognized Negro lodge under a Grand Lodge of one of our States. It is the exception which proves the rule. History tells you how it happened.

"According to our ideas, no woman can be a Freemason. It is unthinkable as to suppose a woman could be a father. But some foreign Masons have made what they call woman Freemasons. Their apostasy doesn't affect any one but themselves. It is too true that some lodges in this country won't have Jews or foreigners in their membership. That is their privilege. But that doesn't make Masonry contradictory; it makes those Masons contradict what they were taught. There is no Masonic reason why a Roman Catholic cannot be a Freemason; the reason they cannot is because their Church forbids them to join oath-bound societies outside of their own. Some Catholics in foreign countries have done so; honor the lodge broad-minded enough to receive them! We do not receive them; we contend that a man owes his allegiance to where his faith is given; if a Catholic applies to us, knowing that his Church forbids it, it is evidence that he is ready to disobey where he has promised obedience. Therefore, we don't want him.

"Masonry opposes the Catholic hierarchy. We defend American institutions from Papal encroachment. It is their organization, their political ambitions we oppose; not that they choose to worship God in ways which are strange to us.

"Masonry is not Christian. It is not Mohammedan. It is not Buddhistic. It is not of any faith or creed. Because some one lodge or Grand Lodge declaims that it is, does not make it so. Masonry does not contradict itself; Masons contradict themselves!

"Men are not perfect. If they were, there would be no need of Masonry. Masonry could not function in a perfect world of perfect men. There would be no use of a system of morality when all men were moral; no need of teaching anything by symbols or any other means if all men were wise. But men are not perfect; they quarrel and disagree and take exceptions to each other's ideas and beliefs. But it is the men, not the Masonry, which contradict!

"Life is all a compromise, my brother. Practical Masonry is a compromise. Never can we all be perfect. And one of the greatest teachings of Masonry is toleration; toleration of the other fellow's idea, his viewpoint, his belief. When you are intolerant of these contradictions, you are yourself a contradiction of Masonic teachings. If I taught you that Masonry contradicted herself, I would be a contradiction!"

"I will not contradict you!" smiled the Young Mason, "unless you say I am not grateful."

Why Symbolism?

"I am puzzled" began the new Master Mason, "over a matter on which I have vainly sought light among my brethren. None gives me a satisfactory answer. We are taught that Masonry teaches through symbols; I want to know why. Why do we not put our truths into plain words? Why do we employ one thing to stand for another thing? Wouldn't Masonry be stronger and better if it was plain instead of 'veiling in allegory' its principles and ethics?"

"Like so many questions which can be answered regarding Masonry,' answered the Old Past Master,' this one may have several answers, all correct."

"Well, what is your answer?" demanded the new Master Mason.

"You will surely admit without argument," answered the Old Past Master, "that man is a triple nature; he is physical, mental and spiritual. He has a body, and senses which bring him into contact with, and translate the meanings of, the physical world of earth, air, fire and water, which is about him. He has a brain and a mind, by which he reasons and understands about the matters physical which he is surrounded. And he has a 'Something Beyond'; you may call it Soul, or Heart, or Spirit, or Imagination as you will, but it is something which is allied to, rather than a part of, reason, and which is connected with the physical side of life only through its sensory contacts.

"Your soul or spirit, my brother, comprehends a language which the brain does not understand. The keenest of minds have striven to make this mystic language plain to reason, without success. If you hear music which brings tears to your eyes and grief or joy to your heart, you are responding to a language your brain does not understand and cannot explain. It is not with your brain that you love your mother, your child or your wife; it is 'Something

Beyond'; and the language with which that love is spoken and understood is not the language of the tongue.

"A symbol is a word in that language. Translate that symbol into words which appeal only to the mind, and the spirit of the word is lost. Words appeal to the mind; meanings not expressed in words appeal to the spirit.

"All that there is in Freemasonry, which can be set down in words on a page, leaves out completely the spirit of the Order. If we depended on words, or ideas alone, the fraternity would not make a universal appeal to all men, since no man has it given to him to appeal to the minds of all other men. But Freemasonry expresses truths which are universal; it expresses them in a universal language, universally understood by all men without words. That language is the language of the symbol, and the symbol is universally understood because it is the means of communication between spirits, souls, hearts.

"Indeed, when we say of Masonry that it is 'universal,' we mean literally; it is of the universe, not merely of the world. If it were possible for an inhabitant of Mars to make and use a telescope which would enable him to see plainly a square mile of the surface of the earth, and if we knew it, and desired by drawing upon that square mile a symbol, to communicate with the inhabitants of Mars, we would choose, undoubtedly, one with as many meanings as possible; one which had a material, a mental and a spiritual meaning. Such a symbol would be the triangle, the square or the circle. Our supposed Martian might respond with a complementary symbol; if we showed him a triangle, he might reply with the 47th problem of Euclid; if we showed him a circle, he might set down 3.141659 (the number by which a diameter multiplied, becomes a circumference). We would find in a symbol a language with which to begin communication, even with all the universe!

"Naturally then, we employ symbols here for heart to speak to heart. Call it soul, mind, spirit, what you will, imagination is its collection of senses. So we must appeal to the imagination when speaking a truth which is neither mental nor physical, and the symbol is the means by which one imagination speaks to another. Nothing else will do; no words can be as effective (unless they are themselves symbols), no teachings expressed in language can be as easily taught or learned by the heart as those which come via the symbol through the imagination. Take from Freemasonry its symbols and you have but the husk; the kernel is gone. He who hears but the words of Freemasonry misses its meaning entirely.

"The symbol has many interpretations. These o not contradict each other; they amplify each other. Thus, the square is a symbol of perfection, of rectitude of conduct, of honor and honesty, of good work. These are all different, and yet allied. The square is not a symbol of wrong, or evil, or meanness or disease! Ten different men may read ten different meanings into a square, and yet each meaning fits with, and belongs to, the other meanings.

"Now ten men have ten different kinds of hearts. Not all have the same power of imagination. They do not all have the same ability to comprehend. So each gets from a symbol what he can. He uses his imagination. He translates to his soul as much of the truth as he is able to make part of him. This the ten cannot do with truths expressed in words. 'Twice two is equal to four' is a truth which must be accepted all at once, as a complete exposition, or not at all. He who can understand but the 'twice' or the 'equal' or the 'four' has no conception of what is being said. But ten men can read ten progressive, different, correct and beautiful meanings into the trowel, and each be right as far as he goes. The man who sees it merely as an instrument which helps to bind, has a part of the meaning. He who finds it a link with operative Masons has another part. The man who sees it as a symbol of man's relationship to Deity, because with it he (spiritually) does the Master's work, has another meaning. All these meanings are right;

when all men know all the meanings the need of Masonry will have passed away.

"To sum up, the reason we must use symbols is because only by them can we speak the language of the spirit, each to each, and because they form an elastic language, which each man reads for himself according to his ability. Symbolism is the only language which is that elastic, and the only one by which the spirit can be touched.

"To suggest that Masonry use any other would be as revolutionary as to remove her Altars, meet in the public square or elect by a majority vote! In other words, Masonry without symbols would not be Masonry; it would be but dogmatic and not very erudite philosophy, of which the world is full as it is, and none of which ever satisfies the heart!"